Praise for
Big Data Demystified

'Before you embark on any kind of big data initiative at your organisation, read this book! It is an essential guide to using data in a practical way that drives results.'

Ian McHenry, CEO, Beyond Pricing

'This is the book we've been missing: big data explained without the complexity! And it will help you to look for big data opportunities in your day-to-day work.'

Marc Salomon, Professor in Decision Sciences and Dean,
University of Amsterdam Business School

'Big data for the rest of us! I have never come across a book that is so full of practical advice, actionable examples and helpful explanations. Read this one book and start executing big data at your workplace tomorrow!'

Tobias Wann, CEO, @Leisure Group

'Dr Stephénson provides an excellent overview of the opportunities and tools that a modern business can exploit in data, while also going deep into the technical, organisational and procedural solutions. This book can be used as a best-practice education for both data analytics n00bs and seasoned professionals looking to identify gaps in data strategy.'

Clancy Childs, Chief Product and Technology Officer,
Dow Jones DNA; Former Product Manager, Google Analytics

Big Data Demystified

Pearson

At Pearson, we have a simple mission: to help people make more of their lives through learning.

We combine innovative learning technology with trusted content and educational expertise to provide engaging and effective learning experiences that serve people wherever and whenever they are learning.

From classroom to boardroom, our curriculum materials, digital learning tools and testing programmes help to educate millions of people worldwide – more than any other private enterprise.

Every day our work helps learning flourish, and wherever learning flourishes, so do people.

To learn more, please visit us at **www.pearson.com/uk**

Big Data Demystified

How to use big data, data science and AI
to make better business decisions and
gain competitive advantage

David Stephenson, PhD

 Pearson

Harlow, England • London • New York • Boston • San Francisco • Toronto • Sydney
Dubai • Singapore • Hong Kong • Tokyo • Seoul • Taipei • New Delhi
Cape Town • São Paulo • Mexico City • Madrid • Amsterdam • Munich • Paris • Milan

Pearson Education Limited
KAO Two
KAO Park
Harlow CM17 9NA
United Kingdom
Tel: +44 (0)1279 623623
Web: www.pearson.com/uk

First edition published 2018 (print and electronic)

ISBN: 978-1-292-21810-6 (print)
       978-1-292-21811-3 (PDF)
       978-1-292-21812-0 (ePub)

British Library Cataloguing-in-Publication Data
A catalogue record for the print edition is available from the British Library

Library of Congress Cataloging-in-Publication Data
A catalog record for the print edition is available from the Library of Congress

10 9 8 7 6 5 4 3 2 1
22 21 20 19 18

Cover design by Two Associates

Print edition typeset in 9.5/13, ITC Giovanni Std by iEnergizer, Aptara® Ltd.
Printed by Ashford Colour Press Ltd, Gosport

NOTE THAT ANY PAGE CROSS REFERENCES REFER TO THE PRINT EDITION

Contents

About the author

David Stephenson consults and speaks internationally in the fields of data science and big data analytics. He completed his PhD at Cornell University and was a professor at the University of Pennsylvania, designing and teaching courses for students in the engineering and Wharton business schools.

David has nearly 20 years of industry experience across Europe and the United States, delivering analytic insights and tools that have guided $10+ billion in business decisions and serving as an expert advisor to top-tier investment, private equity and management consulting firms. He has led global analytics programmes for companies spanning six continents.

David is from the USA but has been living in Amsterdam since 2006. More information and content are available on his company website at www.dsianalytics.com.

Acknowledgements

I would like to thank Eloise Cook at Pearson for her valuable editorial guidance, Uri Weis for comments on the first draft of the text and Matt Gardner for comments on the initial chapters. Thanks also to my father for proofing and providing helpful comments on the entire text. Despite their best efforts, any remaining errors are my own.

Introduction

You often hear the term 'big data', but do you really know what it is and why it's important? Can it make a difference in your organization, improving results and bringing competitive advantage, and is it possible that not utilizing big data puts you at a significant competitive disadvantage?

The goal of this book is to demystify the term 'big data' and to give practical ways for you to leverage this data using data science and machine learning.

The term 'big data' refers to a new class of data: vast, rapidly accumulating quantities, which often do not fit a traditional structure. The term 'big' is an understatement that simply does not do justice to the complexity of the situation. The data we are dealing with is not only bigger than traditional data; it is fundamentally different, as a motorcycle is more than simply a bigger bicycle and an ocean is more than simply a deeper swimming pool. It brings new challenges, presents new opportunities, blurs traditional competitive boundaries and requires a paradigm shift related to how we draw tangible value from data. The ocean of data, combined with the technologies that have been developed to handle it, provide insights at enormous scale and have made possible a new wave of machine learning, enabling computers to drive cars, predict heart attacks better than physicians and master extremely complex games such as **Go** better than any human.

Why is big data a game-changer? As we will see, it allows us to draw much deeper insights from our data, understanding what motivates our customers and what slows down our production lines. In real time, it enables businesses to simultaneously deliver highly personalized experiences to millions of global customers, and it provides the computational power needed for scientific endeavours to analyse billions of data points in fields such as cancer research, astronomy and particle physics. Big data provides both the data and the computational resources that have enabled the recent resurgence in artificial intelligence, particularly with advances in **deep learning**, a methodology that has recently been making global headlines.

Beyond the data itself, researchers and engineers have worked over the past two decades to develop an entire ecosystem of hardware and software solutions for collecting, storing, processing and analysing this abundant data. I refer to these hardware and software tools together as the **big data ecosystem**. This ecosystem allows us to draw immense value from big data for applications in business, science and healthcare. But to use this data, you need to piece together the parts of the big data ecosystem that work best for your applications, and you need to apply appropriate analytic methods to the data – a practice that has come to be known as **data science.**

All in all, the story of big data is much more than simply a story about data and technology. It is about what is already being done in commerce, science and society and what difference it can make for your business. Your decisions must go further than purchasing a technology. In this book, I will outline tools, applications and processes and explain how to draw value from modern data in its many forms.

Most organizations see big data as an integral part of their digital transformation. Many of the most successful organizations are already well along their way in applying big data and data science techniques, including machine learning. Research has shown a strong correlation between big data usage and revenue growth (50 per cent higher revenue growth[1]), and it is not unusual for organizations applying data science techniques to see a 10–20 per cent improvement in **key performance indicators (KPIs)**.

For organizations that have not yet started down the path of leveraging big data and data science, the number one barrier is simply not knowing if the benefits are worth the cost and effort. I hope to make those benefits clear in this book, along the way providing case studies to illustrate the value and risks involved.

In the second half of this book, I'll describe practical steps for creating a data strategy and for getting data projects done within your organization. I'll talk about how to bring the right people together and create a plan for collecting and using data. I'll discuss specific areas in which data science and big data tools can be used within your organization to improve results, and I'll give advice on finding and hiring the right people to carry out these plans.

I'll also talk about additional considerations you'll need to address, such as data governance and privacy protection, with a view to protecting your organization against competitive, reputational and legal risks.

We'll end with additional practical advice for successfully carrying out data initiatives within your organization.

Overview of chapters

Part 1: Big data demystified

Chapter 1: The story of big data

How big data developed into a phenomenon, why big data has become such an important topic over the past few years, where the data is coming from, who is using it and why, and what has changed to make possible today what was not possible in the past.

Chapter 2: Artificial intelligence, machine learning and big data

A brief history of artificial intelligence (AI), how it relates to machine learning, an introduction to neural networks and deep learning, how AI is used today and how it relates to big data, and some words of caution in working with AI.

Chapter 3: Why is big data useful?

How our data paradigm is changing, how big data opens new opportunities and improves established analytic techniques, and what it means to be data-driven, including success stories and case studies.

Chapter 4: Use cases for (big) data analytics

An overview of 20 common business applications of (big) data, analytics and data science, with an emphasis on ways in which big data improves existing analytic methods.

Chapter 5: Understanding the big data ecosystem

Overview of key concepts related to big data, such as open-source code, distributed computing and cloud computing.

Part 2: Making the big data ecosystem work for your organization

Chapter 6: How big data can help guide your strategy

Using big data to guide strategy based on insights into your customers, your product performance, your competitors and additional external factors.

Chapter 7: Forming your strategy for big data and data science

Step-by-step instructions for scoping your data initiatives based on business goals and broad stakeholder input, assembling a project team, determining the most relevant analytics projects and carrying projects through to completion.

Chapter 8: Implementing data science – analytics, algorithms and machine learning

Overview of the primary types of analytics, how to select models and databases, and the importance of agile methods to realize business value.

Chapter 9: Choosing your technologies

Choosing technologies for your big data solution: which decisions you'll need to make, what to keep in mind, and what resources are available to help make these choices.

Chapter 10: Building your team

The key roles needed in big data and data science programmes, and considerations for hiring or outsourcing those roles.

Chapter 11: Governance and legal compliance

Principles in privacy, data protection, regulatory compliance and data governance, and their impact from legal, reputational and internal perspectives. Discussions of PII, linkage attacks and Europe's new privacy regulation (GDPR). Case studies of companies that have gotten into trouble from inappropriate use of data.

Chapter 12: Launching the ship – successful deployment in the organization

Case study of a high-profile project failure. Best practices for making data initiatives successful in your organization, including advice on making your organization more data-driven, positioning your analytics staff within your organization, consolidating data and using resources efficiently.

Part

1

Big data demystified

Chapter

The story of big data

We've always struggled with storing data. Not long ago, our holidays were remembered at a cost of $1 per photo. We saved only the very best TV shows and music recitals, overwriting older recordings. Our computers always ran out of memory.

Newer, cheaper technologies turned up the tap on that data flow. We bought digital cameras, and we linked our computers to networks. We saved more data on less expensive computers, but we still sorted and discarded information continuously. We were frugal with storage, but the data we stored was small enough to manage.

Data started flowing thicker and faster. Technology made it progressively easier for anyone to create data. Roll film cameras gave way to digital video cameras, even on our smartphones. We recorded videos we never replayed.

High-resolution sensors spread through scientific and industrial equipment. More documents were saved in digital format. More significantly, the internet began linking global data silos, creating challenges and opportunities we were ill-equipped to handle. The *coup de grâce* came with the development of crowd-sourced digital publishing, such as YouTube and Facebook, which opened the portal for anyone with a connected digital device to make nearly unlimited contributions to the world's data stores.

But storage was only part of the challenge. While we were rationing our storage, computer scientists were rationing computer processing power. They were writing computer programs to solve problems in science and industry: helping to understand chemical reactions, predict stock market movements and minimize the cost of complicated resource scheduling problems.

Their programs could take days or weeks to finish, and only the most well-endowed organizations could purchase the powerful computers needed to solve the harder problems.

In the 1960s and again in the 1980s, computer scientists were building high hopes for advancements in the field of **machine learning (ML)**, a type of **artificial intelligence (AI)**, but their efforts stalled each time, largely due to limitations in data and technology.

In summary, our ability to draw value from data was severely limited by the technologies of the twentieth century.

What changed towards the start of the twenty-first century?

There were several key developments towards the start of the twenty-first century. One of the most significant originated in Google. Created to navigate the overwhelming data on the newly minted world wide web, Google was all about big data. Its researchers soon developed ways to make normal computers work together like supercomputers, and in 2003 they published these results in a paper which formed the basis for a **software framework** known as **Hadoop**. Hadoop became the bedrock on which much of the world's initial big data efforts would be built.

The concept of 'big data' incubated quietly in the technology sector for nearly a decade before becoming mainstream. The breakthrough into management circles seemed to happen around 2011, when McKinsey published their report, *'Big data: The next frontier for innovation, competition, and productivity.'*[2] The first public talk I gave on big data was at a designated 'big data' conference in London the next year (2012), produced by a media company seizing the opportunity to leverage a newly trending topic.

But even before the McKinsey paper, large data-driven companies such as eBay were already developing internal solutions for fundamental big data challenges. By the time of McKinsey's 2011 publication, Hadoop was already five years old and the University of California at Berkeley had open-sourced their **Spark** framework, the Hadoop successor that leveraged inexpensive **RAM** to process big data much more quickly than Hadoop.

Let's look at why data has grown so rapidly over the past few years and why the topic 'big data' has become so prominent.

Why so much data?

The volume of data we are committing to digital memory is undergoing explosive growth for two reasons:

1. The proliferation of devices that generate digital data: ubiquitous personal computers and mobile phones, scientific sensors, and the literally billions of sensors across the expanding **Internet of Things (IoT)** (see Figure 1.1).
2. The rapidly plummeting cost of digital storage.

The proliferation of devices that generate digital data

Technology that creates and collects data has become cheap, and it is everywhere. These computers, smartphones, cameras, RFID (radio-frequency identification), movement sensors, etc., have found their way into the hands of the mass consumer market as well as those of scientists, industries and governments. Sometimes we intentionally create data, such as when we take videos or post to websites, and sometimes we create data unintentionally, leaving a digital footprint on a webpage that we browse, or carrying smartphones

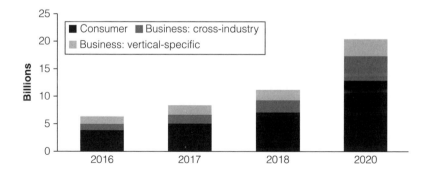

Figure 1.1 Number of IoT devices by category.[3]

that send geospatial information to network providers. Sometimes the data doesn't relate to us at all, but is a record of machine activity or scientific phenomena. Let's look at some of the main sources and uses of the data modern technology is generating.

Content generation and self-publishing

What does it take to get your writing published? A few years ago, it took a printing press and a network of booksellers. With the internet, you only needed the skills to create a web page. Today, anyone with a Facebook or Twitter account can instantly publish content with worldwide reach. A similar story has played out for films and videos. Modern technology, particularly the internet, has completely changed the nature of publishing and has facilitated a massive growth in human-generated content.

Self-publishing platforms for the masses, particularly Facebook, YouTube and Twitter, threw open the floodgates of mass-produced data. Anyone could easily post content online, and the proliferation of mobile devices, particularly those capable of recording and uploading video, further lowered the barriers. Since nearly everyone now has a personal device with a high-resolution video camera and continuous internet access, the data uploads are enormous. Even children easily upload limitless text or video to the public domain.

YouTube, one of the most successful self-publishing platforms, is possibly the single largest consumer of corporate data storage today. Based on previously published statistics, it is estimated that YouTube is adding approximately 100 **petabytes (PB)** of new data per year, generated from several hundred hours of video uploaded each minute. We are also watching a tremendous amount of video online, on YouTube, Netflix and similar streaming services. Cisco recently estimated that it would take more than 5 million years to watch the amount of video that will cross global IP (internet protocol) networks each month in 2020.

Consumer activity

When I visit a website, the owner of that site can see what information I request from the site (search words, filters selected, links clicked). The site can also use the **JavaScript** on my browser to record how I interact with the page: when I scroll down or hover my mouse over an item. Websites use these details to better understand visitors, and a site might record details for several hundred categories of online actions (searches, clicks, scrolls, hovers, etc.). Even if I never log in and the site doesn't know who I am, the insights are valuable. The more information the site gathers about its visitor base, the better it can optimize marketing efforts, landing pages and product mix.

Mobile devices produce even heavier digital trails. An application installed on my smartphone may have access to the device sensors, including GPS (global positioning system). Since many people always keep their smartphones near them, the phones maintain very accurate data logs of the location and activity cycles of their owner. Since the phones are typically in constant communication with cell towers and Wi-Fi routers, third parties may also see the owners' locations. Even companies with brick-and-mortar shops are increasingly using signals from smartphones to track the physical movement of customers within their stores.

Many companies put considerable effort into analysing these digital trails, particularly e-commerce companies wanting to better understand online visitors. In the past, these companies would discard most data, storing only the key events (e.g. completed sales), but many websites are now storing all data from each online visit, allowing them to look back and ask detailed questions. The scale of this customer journey data is typically several **gigabytes (GB)** per day for smaller websites and several **terabytes (TB)** per day for larger sites. We'll return to the benefits of analysing customer journey data in later chapters.

We are generating data even when we are offline, through our phone conversations or when moving past video cameras in shops, city streets, airports or roadways. Security companies and intelligence agencies rely heavily on such data. In fact, the largest consumer of data storage today is quite likely the United States' National Security Agency (NSA). In August 2014, the NSA completed construction of a massive data centre in Bluffdale, Utah, codenamed *Bumblehive*, at a cost somewhere between 1 and 2 billion dollars. Its actual storage capacity is classified, but the governor of Utah told reporters in 2012 that it would be, 'the first facility in the world expected to gather and house a **yottabyte**'.

Machine data and the Internet of Things (IoT)

Machines never tire of generating data, and the number of connected machines is growing at a rapid pace. One of the more
mind-blowing things you can do in the next five minutes is to
check out Cisco's Visual Networking Index™, which recently estimated that global IP traffic will reach over two **zettabytes** per year
by 2020.

We may hit a limit in the number of mobile phones and personal
computers we use, but we'll continue adding networked processors
to devices around us. This huge network of connected sensors and
processors is known as the **Internet of Things (IoT)**. It includes the
smart energy meters appearing in our homes, the sensors in our
cars that help us drive and sometimes communicate with our
insurance companies, the sensors deployed to monitor soil, water,
fauna or atmospheric conditions, the digital control systems used
to monitor and optimize factory equipment, etc. The number of
such devices stood at approximately 5 billion in 2015 and has been
estimated to reach between 20 and 50 billion by 2020.

Scientific research

Scientists have been pushing the boundaries of data transport and
data processing technologies. I'll start with an example from particle physics.

Case study
The Large Hadron Collider (particle physics)

One of the most important recent events in physics was wit-
nessed on 4 July 2012: the discovery of the Higgs boson particle,
also known as 'the God particle'. After 40 years of searching,
researchers finally identified the particle using the Large Had-
ron Collider (LHC), the world's largest machine[4] (see Figure 1.2).
The massive LHC lies within a tunnel 17 miles (27 km) in circum-
ference, stretching over the Swiss–French border. Its 150 million
sensors deliver data from experiments 30 million times per

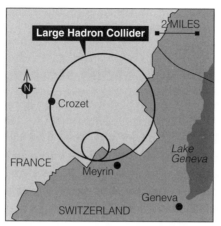

Figure 1.2 The world's largest machine.[5]

second. This data is further filtered to a few hundred points of interest per second. The total annual data flow reaches 50 PB, roughly the equivalent of 500 years of full HD-quality movies. It is the poster child of big data research in physics.

Case study
The Square Kilometre Array (astronomy)

On the other side of the world lies the Australian Square Kilometre Array Pathfinder (ASKAP), a radio telescope array of 36 parabolic antennas, each 12 metres in diameter[6] and spanning 4000 square metres. Twelve of the 36 antennas were activated in October 2016[7], and the full 36, when commissioned, are expected to produce data at a rate of over 7.5 TB per second[8] (one month's worth of HD movies per second). Scientists are planning a larger Square Kilometre Array (SKA), which will be spread over several continents and be 100 times larger than the ASKAP. This may be the largest single data collection device ever conceived.

All of this new data presents abundant opportunities, but let's return now to our fundamental problem, the cost of processing and storing that data.

The plummeting cost of disk storage

There are two main types of computer storage: disk (e.g. hard drive) and random access memory (RAM). Disk storage is like a filing cabinet next to your desk. There may be a lot of space, but it takes time to store and retrieve the information. RAM is like the space on top of your desk. There is less space, but you can grab what's there very quickly. Both types of storage are important for handling big data.

Disk storage has been cheaper, so we put most data there. The cost of disk storage has been the limiting factor for data archiving. With a gigabyte (GB) of hard drive storage costing $200,000 in 1980, it's not hard to understand why we stored so little. By 1990, the cost had dropped to $9000 per GB, still expensive but falling fast. By the year 2000, it had fallen to an amazing $10 per GB. This was a tipping point, as we'll see. By 2017, a GB of hard drive storage cost less than 3 cents (see Figure 1.3).

This drop in storage cost brought interesting consequences. It became cheaper to store useless data rather than take time to filter

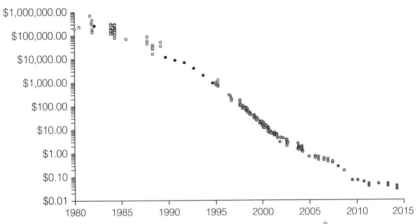

Figure 1.3 Historic cost of disk storage per GB (log scale).[9]

and discard it (think about all the duplicate photos you've never deleted). We exchanged the challenge of managing scarcity for the challenge of managing over-abundant data, a fundamentally different problem. This story repeats itself across business, science and nearly every sector that relies on digital data for decisions or operations.

Online companies had previously kept a fraction of web data and discarded the rest. Now these companies are keeping all data: every search, scroll and click, stored with time stamps to allow future reconstruction of each customer visit, just in case the data might prove useful later.

But exceptionally large hard drives were still exceptionally expensive, and many companies needed these. They could not simply buy additional smaller, inexpensive drives, as the data needed to be processed in a holistic manner (you can divide a load of bricks between several cars, but you need a truck to move a piano). For organizations to take full advantage of the drop in hard drive prices, they would need to find a way to make a small army of mid-sized hard drives operate together as if they were one very large hard drive.

Google's researchers saw the challenge and the opportunity and set about developing the solution that would eventually become Hadoop. It was a way to link many inexpensive computers and make them function like a super computer. Their initial solution leveraged disk storage, but soon the attention turned to RAM, the faster but more expensive storage media.

The plummeting cost of RAM

Disk (hard drive) storage is great for archiving data, but it is slow, requiring time for computer processors to read and write the data as they process it. If you picture working at a very small desk next to an enormous filing cabinet, constantly retrieving and refiling papers to complete your work on this small desk, you'll quickly realize the benefits of a larger desk. RAM storage is like that desk space. It's much faster to work with, which is a significant benefit when processing the huge volumes of high-velocity

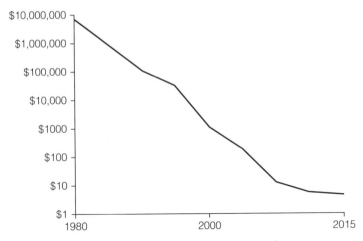

Figure 1.4 Historic cost of RAM per GB (log scale).
Source: http://www.statisticbrain.com/average-historic-price-of-ram/

data that the world was producing. But RAM is much more expensive than disk storage. Its price was also falling, but it had more distance to cover

How much more expensive is RAM storage? In 1980, when a GB of hard drive cost $200k, a GB of RAM cost $6 million. By the year 2000, when hard drives were at $15 and could be used for scalable big data solutions, a GB of RAM was well above $1000, prohibitively expensive for large-scale applications (see Figure 1.4).

By 2010, however, RAM had fallen to $12 per GB, the price at which disk storage had seen its tipping point back in 2000. It was time for Berkeley labs to release a new RAM-based big data framework. This computational framework, which they called Spark, used large amounts of RAM to process big data up to 100 times faster than Hadoop's **MapReduce** processing model.

The plummeting cost of processing power

The cost of computer processing has also plummeted, bringing new opportunities to solve really hard problems and to draw value from the massive amounts of new data that we have started collecting (see Figure 1.5).

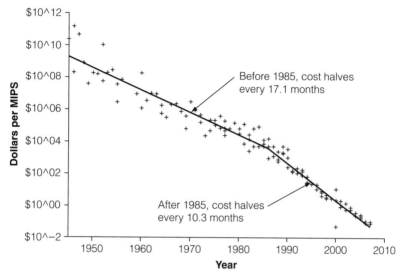

Figure 1.5 Historic cost of processing power (log scale).[10]

Why did big data become such a hot topic?

Over the last 15 years, we've come to realize that big data is an opportunity rather than a problem. McKinsey's 2011 report spoke directly to the CEOs, elaborating on the value of big data for five applications (healthcare, retail, manufacturing, the public sector and personal location data). The report predicted big data could raise KPIs by 60 per cent and estimated hundreds of billions of dollars of added value per sector. The term 'big data' became the buzzword heard around the world, drawn out of the corners of technology and cast into the executive spotlight.

With so many people talking so much about a topic they so little understood, many quickly grew jaded about the subject. But big data became such a foundational concept that Gartner, which had added big data to their **Gartner Hype Cycle** for Emerging Technologies in 2012, made the unusual decision to completely remove it from the Hype Cycle in 2015, thus acknowledging that big data had become so foundational as to warrant henceforth being referred to simply as 'data' (see Figure 1.6).

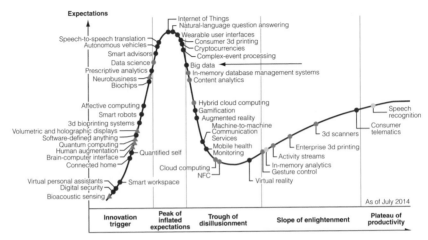

Figure 1.6 Gartner Hype Cycle for Emerging Technologies, 2014.

Organizations are now heavily dependent on big data. But why such widespread adoption?

- **Early adopters,** such as Google and Yahoo, risked significant investments in hardware and software development. These companies paved the way for others, demonstrating commercial success and sharing computer code.

- **The second wave** of adopters did much of the hardest work. They could benefit from the examples of the early adopters and leverage some shared code but still needed to make significant investments in hardware and develop substantial internal expertise.

Today, we have reached a point where we have the role models and the tools for nearly any organization to start leveraging big data.

Let's start with looking at some role models who have inspired us in the journey.

Successful big data pioneers

Google's first mission statement was 'to organize the world's information and make it universally accessible and useful.' Its valuation of $23 million only eight years later demonstrated to the world the value of mastering big data.

It was Google that released the 2003 paper that formed the basis of Hadoop. In January 2006, Yahoo made the decision to implement Hadoop in their systems.[11] Yahoo was also doing quite well in those days, with a stock price that had slowly tripled over the previous five years.

Around the time that Yahoo was implementing Hadoop, eBay was working to rethink how it handled the volume and variety of its customer journey data. Since 2002, eBay had been utilizing a **massively parallel processing (MPP)** Teradata database for reporting and analytics. The system worked very well, but storing the entire web logs was prohibitively expensive on such a proprietary system.

eBay's infrastructure team worked to develop a solution combining several technologies and capable of storing and analysing tens of petabytes of data. This gave eBay significantly more detailed customer insights and played an important role in their platform development, translating directly into revenue gains.

Open-source software has levelled the playing field for software developers

Computers had become cheaper, but they still needed to be programmed to operate in unison if they were to handle big data (such as coordinating several small cars to move a piano, instead of one truck). Code needed to be written for basic functionality, and additional code needed to be written for more specialized tasks. This was a substantial barrier to any big data project, and it is where open-source software played such an important role.

Open-source software is software which is made freely available for anyone to use and modify (subject to some restrictions). Because big data software such as Hadoop was open-sourced, developers everywhere could share expertise and build off each other's code.

Hadoop is one of many big data tools that have been open-sourced. As of 2017, there are roughly 100 projects related to big data or Hadoop in the **Apache Software Foundation** alone (we'll discuss the Apache Foundation later). Each of these projects solves a new challenge or solves an old challenge in a new way. For example, Apache **Hive** allows companies to use Hadoop as a large database, and Apache **Kafka** provides messaging between machines. New projects are continually being released to Apache, each one addressing a specific need and further lowering the barrier for subsequent entrants into the big data ecosystem.

Keep in mind

Most of the technology you'll need for extracting value from big data is already readily available. If you're just starting out with big data, leverage as much existing technology as possible.

Affordable hardware and open-sourced software were lowering the barrier for companies to start using big data. But the problem remained that buying and setting up computers for a big data system was an expensive, complicated and risky process, and companies were uncertain how much hardware to purchase. What they needed was access to computing resources without long-term commitment.

Cloud computing has made it easy to launch and scale initiatives

Cloud computing is essentially renting all or part of an offsite computer. Many companies are already using one or more **public cloud** services: AWS, Azure, Google Cloud, or a local provider. Some companies maintain **private clouds**, which are computing resources that are maintained centrally within the company and made available to business units on demand. Such private clouds allow efficient use of shared resources.

Cloud computing can provide hardware or software solutions. **Salesforce** began in 1999 as a Software as a Service (SaaS), a form of cloud computing. Amazon Web Services (AWS) launched its Infrastructure as a Service (IaaS) in 2006, first renting storage and a few months later renting entire servers. Microsoft launched its cloud computing platform, Azure, in 2010, and Google launched Google Cloud in 2011.

Cloud computing solved a pain point for companies uncertain of their computing and storage needs. It allowed companies to undertake big data initiatives without the need for large capital expenditures, and it allowed them to immediately scale existing initiatives up or down. In addition, companies could move the cost of big data infrastructure from **CapEx** to **OpEx**.

The costs of cloud computing are falling, and faster networks allow remote machines to integrate seamlessly. Overall, cloud computing has brought agility to big data, making it possible for companies to experiment and scale without the cost, commitment and wait-time of purchasing dedicated computers.

With scalable data storage and compute power in place, the stage was set for researchers to once again revisit a technology that had stalled in the 1960s and again in the 1980s: artificial intelligence.

Takeaways

- Modern technology has given us tools to produce much more digital information than ever before.
- The dramatic fall in the cost of digital storage allows us to keep virtually unlimited amounts of data.
- Technology pioneers have developed and shared software that enables us to create substantial business value from today's data.

Ask yourself

- How are organizations in your sector already using big data technologies? Consider your competitors as well as companies in other sectors.
- What data would be useful to you if you could store and analyse it as you'd like? Think, for example, of traffic to your website(s), audio and video recordings, or sensor readings.
- What is the biggest barrier to your use of big data: technology, skill sets or use-cases?

Chapter

Artificial intelligence, machine learning and big data

On 11 May 1997, an IBM computer named *Deep Blue* made history by defeating Garry Kasparov, the reigning world chess champion, in a match in New York City. Deep Blue won using raw computing muscle, evaluating up to 200 million moves per second as it referred to a list of rules it had been programmed to follow. Its programmers even adjusted its programming between games. But Deep Blue was a one-trick pony, soon dismantled. Computers were far from out-performing humans at most elementary tasks or in more complicated games, such as the Chinese game of **Go**, where there are more possible game states than atoms in the universe (see Figure 2.1).

Figure 2.1 A Go gameboard.

Fast forward 19 years to a match in Seoul, Korea, when a program named *AlphaGo* defeated reigning world Go champion Lee Sedol. Artificial intelligence had not simply improved in the 19 years since Deep Blue, it had become fundamentally different. Whereas Deep Blue had improved through additional, explicit instructions and faster processors, AlphaGo was learning on its own. It first studied expert moves and then it practised against itself. Even the developers of AlphaGo couldn't explain the logic behind certain moves that it made. It had taught itself to make them.

What are artificial intelligence and machine learning?

Artificial intelligence (AI) is a broad term for when a machine can respond intelligently to its environment. We interact with AI in Apple's Siri, Amazon's Echo, self-driving cars, online chat-bots and gaming opponents. AI also helps in less obvious ways. It is filtering spam from our inboxes, correcting our spelling mistakes, and deciding what posts appear on top of our social media feeds. AI has a broad range of applications, including image recognition, natural language processing, medical diagnosis, robotic movements, fraud detection and much more.

Machine learning (ML) is when a machine keeps improving its performance, even after you've stopped programming it. ML is what makes most AI work so well, especially when there is abundant training data. Deep Blue was rule-based. It was AI without machine learning. AlphaGo used machine learning and gained its proficiency by first **training** on a large dataset of expert moves and then playing additional games against itself to learn what did or didn't work. Since machine learning techniques improve with more data, big data amplifies machine learning. Most AI headlines today and almost all the AI I'll discuss in this book will be applications of machine learning.

The origins of AI

Researchers have been developing AI methods since the 1950s. Many techniques used today are several decades old, originating in the self-improving **algorithms** developed in the research labs of MIT's Marvin Minsky and Stanford's John McCarthy.

AI and ML hit several false starts. Researchers had high expectations, but computers were limited and initial results were disappointing. By the early 1970s, what was termed 'the first AI winter' had set in, lasting through the end of the decade.

Enthusiasm for AI resurfaced in the 1980s, particularly following industry success with **expert systems.** The US, UK and Japanese governments invested hundreds of millions of dollars in university and government research labs, while corporations spent similar amounts on in-house AI departments. An industry of hardware and software companies grew to support AI.

The AI bubble soon burst again. The supporting hardware market collapsed, expert systems became too expensive to maintain and extensive investments proved disappointing. In 1987, the US government drastically cut AI funding, and the second AI winter began.

Why the recent resurgence of AI?

AI picked up momentum again in the mid-1990s, partly due to the increasing power of supercomputers. Deep Blue's 1997 chess victory was actually a rematch. It had lost 15 months earlier, after which IBM gave it a major hardware upgrade.[12] With twice the processing power, it won the rematch using brute computational force. Although it had used specialized hardware, and although its application was very narrow, Deep Blue had demonstrated the increasing power of AI.

Big data gave an even greater boost to AI with two key developments:

1. We started amassing huge amounts of data that could be used for machine learning.
2. We created software that would allow normal computers to work together with the power of a super-computer.

Powerful machine learning methods could now run on affordable hardware and could feast on massive amounts of **training data.**

As an indication of scale, ML applications today may run on networks of several hundred thousand machines.

One especially well-publicized machine learning technique that is increasingly used today is **artificial neural networks,** a technique recently extended to larger (deeper) networks and branded as deep learning. This technique contributed to AlphaGo's victory in 2016.

Artificial neural networks and deep learning

Artificial neural networks (ANN) have been around since the late 1950s. They are collections of very simple building blocks pieced together to form larger networks. Each block performs only a few basic calculations, but the whole network can be 'trained' to assist with complicated tasks: label photos, interpret documents, drive a car, play a game, etc. Figure 2.2 gives examples of ANN architectures.

Artificial neural networks are so named because of their similarity to the connected neurons within the animal brain. They function as pattern recognition tools, similar to the early layers of our mind's visual cortex but not comparable with the parts of our brains that handle cognitive reasoning.

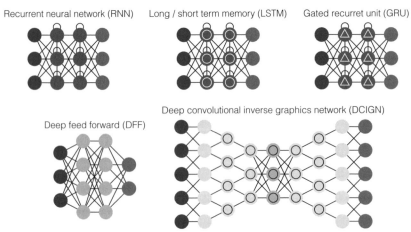

Figure 2.2 Examples of artificial neural network architectures.[13]

The challenge of building an ANN is in choosing an appropriate network model (architecture) for the basic building blocks and then training the network for the desired task.

The trained model is deployed to a computer, a smartphone or even a chip embedded within production equipment. There are an increasing number of tools available to facilitate this process of building, training and deploying ANNs. These include Caffe, developed by Berkley Vision Lab, TensorFlow, developed within Google and released to Apache in November 2015, Theano and others.

'Training' an ANN, involves feeding it millions of labelled examples. To train an ANN to recognize animals, for example, I need to show it millions of pictures and label the pictures with the names of the animals they contain. If all goes well, the trained ANN will then be able to tell me which animals appear in new, unlabelled photos. During the training, the network itself does not change, but the strength of the various connections between the 'neurons' is adjusted to make the model more accurate.

Larger, more complex ANNs can produce models that perform better, but they can take much longer to train. The layered networks are now generally much deeper, hence the rebranding of ANNs as 'deep learning'. Using them requires big data technologies.

ANNs can be applied to a broad range of problems. Before the era of big data, researchers would say that neural networks were 'the second-best way to solve any problem'. This has changed. ANNs now provide some of the best solutions. In addition to improving image recognition, language translation and spam filtering, Google has incorporated ANNs into core search functionality with the implementation of RankBrain in 2015. Rank-Brain, a neural network for search, has proven to be the biggest improvement to ranking quality Google has seen in several years. It has, according to Google, become the third most important of the hundreds of factors that determine search ranking.[14]

> ### Case study
> ### The world's premier image recognition challenge
>
> The premier challenge in image recognition is the annual Ima-geNet Large Scale Visual Recognition Challenge (ILSVRC), in which global research teams compete to build machine learning programs to label over 14 million images. An ANN won the challenge for the first time in 2012, and in a very impressive way. Whereas the best classification error rate for earlier ML algorithms had been 26 per cent, the ANN had a classification error rate of only 15 per cent.
>
> ANNs won every subsequent competition. In 2014, the Goog-LeNet program won with an error rate of only 6.7 per cent using an ANN with 22 layers and several million artificial neurons. This network was three times deeper than that of the 2012 winner, and, in comparison with the number of neurons in the animal brain, their network was slightly ahead of honey bees but still behind frogs.
>
> By 2016, the winning ML algorithm (CUImage) had reduced the classification error to under 3 per cent using an **ensemble** of AI methods, including an ANN with 269 layers (10× deeper than the 2014 winner).

How AI helps analyse big data

Most big data is **unstructured data,** including images, text documents and web logs. We store these in raw form and extract detailed information when needed.

Many traditional analytic methods rely on data that is structured into fields such as *age, gender, address,* etc. To better fit a model, we often create additional data fields, such as *average spend per visit* or *time since last purchase,* a process known as **feature engineering.**

Certain AI methods do not require feature selection and are especially useful for data without clearly defined features. For example, an AI method can learn to identify a cat in a photo just by studying photos of cats, without being taught concepts such as cat faces, ears or whiskers.

Some words of caution

Despite early enthusiasm, the AI we have today is still 'narrow AI'. Each is only useful for the specific application for which it was designed and trained. Deep learning has brought marginal improvements to narrow AI, but what is needed for full AI is a substantially different tool set.

Gary Marcus, a research psychologist at New York University and co-founder of Geometric Intelligence (later acquired by Uber), describes three fundamental problems with deep learning.[15]

1. There will always be bizarre results, particularly when there is insufficient training data. For example, even as AI achieves progressively more astounding accuracy in recognizing images, we continue to see photos tagged with labels bearing no resemblance to the photo, as illustrated in Figure 2.3

A refrigerator filled with lots of food and drinks

Figure 2.3 Example of AI failure.[16]

Figure 2.4 Dog or ostrich?

Or consider Figure 2.4 above. By modifying the image of a dog in the left-hand image in ways that the human eye cannot detect, researchers fooled the best AI program of 2012 into thinking the image on the right was an ostrich.[17]

2. It is very difficult to engineer deep learning processes. They are difficult to debug, revise incrementally and verify.

3. There is no real progress in language understanding or causal reasoning. A program can identify a man and a car in a photo, but it won't wonder, 'Hey, how is that man holding the car above his head?'

Keep in mind

Artificial intelligence is still limited to addressing specific tasks with clear goals. Each application needs a specially designed and trained AI program.

Remember also that AI is very dependent on large quantities of diverse, labelled data and that AI trained with insufficient data will make more mistakes. We've already seen self-driving cars make critical errors when navigating unusual (e.g. untrained) conditions. Our tolerance for inaccuracy in such applications is extremely low.

AI often requires a value system. A self-driving car must know that running over people is worse than running off the road.

Commercial systems must balance revenue and risk reduction with customer satisfaction.

Applications of AI in medicine bring their own promises and pitfalls. A team at Imperial College London has recently developed AI that diagnoses pulmonary hypertension with 80 per cent accuracy, significantly higher than the 60 per cent accuracy typical among cardiologists. Application of such technology, though, brings before us some complicated issues, as we'll discuss later.[18]

AI applications have captured headlines over the past few years, and will doubtless continue to do so. I'll talk more about AI in Chapter 8, when I discuss choosing **analytic models** that fit your business challenges. But AI is just one of many analytic tools in our tool chest, and its scope is still limited. Let's step back now and consider the bigger picture of how big data can bring value through a wider set of tools and in a broad range of applications.

Takeaways

- AI has been actively studied for 60 years, but has twice gone through winters of disillusionment.
- Much of AI involves machine learning, where the program self-learns from examples rather than simply following explicit instructions.
- Big data is a natural catalyst for machine learning.
- Deep learning, a modern enhancement of an older method known as neural networks, is used in much of today's AI technology.
- AI programs are limited in scope and will always make non-intuitive errors.

Ask yourself

- Where in your organization do you have large amounts of labelled data that could be used for training a machine learning program, such as recognizing patterns in pictures or text, or predicting next customer action based on previous actions?

- If you've already started an AI project in your organization, how much greater is its estimated **return on investment (ROI)** than its cost? If you multiply the estimated chance of success by the estimated ROI, you should get a number exceeding the estimated cost.

Chapter

3

'Big data is why Amazon's recommendations work so well. Big data is what tunes search and helps us find what we need. Big data is what makes web and mobile intelligent' —*Greg Linden, pioneering data scientist at Amazon.*[19]

Why is big data useful?

The big data ecosystem fundamentally changes what you can do with data, and it fundamentally changes how you should think about data.

Completely new ways to use data

We are doing things today that we could not have done without big data technologies. Some of these applications are recreational, while some are foundational to our understanding of science and healthcare.

Big data was what enabled scientists to collect and analyse the massive amounts of data that led to the discovery of the Higgs boson at Europe's enormous CERN research facility in 2012. It is allowing astronomers to operate telescopes of unprecedented size. It has brought cancer research forward by decades.[20]

The quantity of training data and the technologies developed to process big data have together breathed new life into the field of artificial intelligence, enabling computers to win at *Jeopardy* (IBM's Watson computer), master very complicated games (Deep-Mind's AlphaGo) and recognize human speech better than professional transcriptionists (Microsoft Research).[21]

The ability of search engines to return relevant results from millions of sources relies on big data tools. Even the ability of mid-sized e-commerce sites to return relevant results from their own inventories relies on big data tools such as **Solr** or **Elastic Search.**

Data and analytics were extremely useful before the recent explosion of data, and 'small data' will continue to be valuable. But some problems can only be solved using big data tools, and many can be solved better using big data tools.

A new way of thinking about data

Big data changes your data paradigm. Instead of rationing storage and discarding potentially valuable data, you retain all data and promote its use. By storing raw data in **data lakes,** you keep all options for future questions and applications.

Consider a simple illustration. Suppose I develop an interest in Tesla cars and decide to count the Teslas I see for one month. After the month, I have a number. But if someone asks me for details about colour, time of day, or perhaps another type of vehicle, I'll need another month before I can give an answer. If I had instead kept a video camera on my car during the first month and had saved all my recordings, I could answer any new questions with data I already had.

Following a data-driven approach

W. Edward Deming, the American engineer who worked to re-invigorate Japanese industry in the 1950s, is often credited for the quote, 'In God we trust; all others bring data.' Whereas some organizations are led by the intuition of their leaders or diligently adhere to established practices, data-driven organizations prioritize data in making decisions and measuring success. Such a data-driven approach was instrumental in Bill Bratton's leadership of the NYPD during the 1990s, when he introduced the CompStat system to help reduce crime in New York City.[22]

In practice, we all operate using a blend of intuition, habit and data, but if you follow a data-driven approach, you will back up your intuition with data and actively develop the tools and talent required to analyse your data.

Data insights

Challenge your assumptions and ask for supporting data. For example, find data showing if your regular promotions are boosting revenue or are simply loss-makers. Track how customer segments respond to different product placements. Find out why they do or don't come back.

Case study
Tesco's Clubcard

Some organizations are natively data-driven. Others undergo a data transformation. British supermarket giant Tesco is an example of the latter. With the help of external analysts, Tesco experienced tremendous success adopting a data-driven approach to customer relations and marketing, fuelled by the data from their Tesco Clubcard. The chairman, Ian MacLaurin, amazed at the analysts' insights, said, 'You know more about my customers in three months than I know in 30 years'.

This period of data-driven growth brought Tesco's market share from 18 per cent in 1994 to 25 per cent in 2000, as shown in Figure 3.1.[23,24] Its management would later say that data had guided nearly all key business decisions during that time, reducing the risk of launching bold initiatives, and providing an extremely clear sense of direction in decision making.

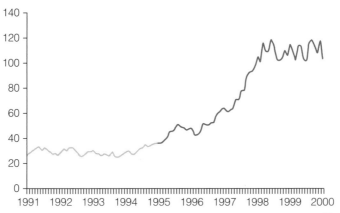

Figure 3.1 Tesco share price (Clubcard launched Q1 1995).[25]

Analysis

Some insights jump out from data. Others you'll have to dig for, perhaps using statistical methods for forecasts or correlations. Our next case study illustrates such a process.

Case study
Target's marketing to expecting mothers

In 2002, when big data technology was still incubating in Silicon Valley, Target Corporation was initiating a data-driven effort that would bring it significant revenue, along with a certain amount of unwelcomed publicity.

Target, the second largest discount retailer in the United States, was struggling to gain market share from Walmart. Target had a brilliant idea, an idea that would require creative use of data.

Professor Alan Andreasen had published a paper in the 1980s demonstrating that buying habits are more likely to change at major life events. For Target, the customer event with perhaps the greatest spending impact would be the birth of a child. Target launched a project to flag pregnant shoppers based on recent purchases, with the goal of marketing baby products to these shoppers at well-timed points in the pregnancy.

Target's analysts carefully studied all available data, including sales records, birth registries and third-party information. Within a few months, they had developed statistical models that could identify pregnant shoppers with high accuracy based solely on what products they were purchasing, even pinpointing their due dates to within a small window.

One year later, an angry father stormed into a Target store outside of Minneapolis, demanding to talk to a manager: 'My daughter got this in the mail!' he said. 'She's still in high school, and you're sending her coupons for baby clothes and cribs? Are you trying to encourage her to get pregnant?' The father soon learned the girl was actually pregnant. The story made headlines, and the world marvelled at how Target had hit a financial gold mine and a PR landmine.

Target saw 20 per cent year-over-year annual growth during these years (2002–2005), growth which they attributed to 'heightened focus on items and categories that appeal to specific guest segments, such as mom and baby.'[26] The world took notice. Target had adopted an analytics-driven approach to marketing, and it had resulted in substantial revenue growth.

Neither the Target nor the Tesco case studies involved what we today call big data, but both brought double-digit growth rates. Target and Tesco took all the information in their systems and added data acquired from third parties. They placed this data in the hands of trained analysts and used the results to steer their operations.

Such data-driven approaches are still bringing success to many companies today. What's changed is that you now have access to new types of data and better tooling.

Better data tooling

Data brings insights. Your ability to archive and analyse so much potentially relevant data lets you find answers quickly and become extremely agile in your business planning. It's disruptive technology.

More data generally enables better analysis. It improves some analysis and completely transforms others. It's like adding power tools to a set of hand tools. Some jobs you can do better, and some that were previously not feasible suddenly become feasible.

In this next section, I'll show some ways big data makes traditional analytics better.

Data: the more the better

You'll want to collect as much data as possible to do your analysis: more types of data and greater quantities of each type.

There is a fundamental principle of analytics that 'more data beats better models'. The strength of your analysis depends on:

1. Discovering what data is most meaningful.
2. Selecting an analytic tool appropriate to the task.
3. Having enough data to make the analysis work.

The reason you'll want to develop big data capabilities is that big data gives you additional types of data (such as customer journey data) for the first dependency and additional quantities of data for the third dependency.

> ## Keep in mind
>
> Update your existing statistical and analytic models to incorporate new data sources, particularly big data such as web traffic, social media, customer support logs, audio and video recordings and various sensor data.

Additional types of data

To illustrate, imagine an insurer calculating the premium for your car insurance. If the insurer knows only your home address, age and car model, they can make a rough estimate of your risk level. Telling the insurer how far you drive each year would give more insight, as more driving means more risk. Telling where and when you drive would give even more insight into your risk. The insurance company will benefit more from getting the additional data than it would from improving its risk model with the original, limited data.

In a similar way, big data provides additional types of data. It gives detailed sensor information to track product performance for machines. It allows us to record and analyse deceleration rates for cars equipped with monitoring devices. It allows us to manage massive volumes of audio and video data, social media activity and online customer journey data.

The value of customer journey data

Customer journey data is an extremely valuable type of big data. Tesco's customer analysis in the late 1990s used demographic information (age, gender, family profile, address) and purchase data. This was a lot of data at the time, considering their limited storage media, and it was sufficient for insights into purchase patterns of customer segments. The resulting insights were valuable for marketing, product selection and pricing, but they gave a two-dimensional view of a three-dimensional world.

Tesco only saw what happened when the customer reached the checkout queue. The data we have today is much richer.

Although traditional web analytics gives you a two-dimensional view, with summary statistics such as traffic volume and conversion events (e.g. purchases), the complete web logs (the big data) will tell you:

- What marketing effort sent each customer to your site: Facebook, Google, an email campaign, a paid advertisement?

- What was top-of-mind when each customer entered? You might see the link that brought them or the first search term used onsite.

- What is most important to each customer? You'll see which filters the customer (de-) selects and the sort order chosen (increasing or decreasing price, rating, etc.). Knowing this can make a significant difference in how you approach each customer during the rest of their online visit.

- What alternate products each customer considered before making a purchase. With the online customer journey, you can analyse **micro-conversions** that signal when you've captured the customer's interest. Particularly for expensive items with infrequent sales, you'll want to understand how items are capturing the interest of your visitors, and you'll use these insights in deciding how to sell to future visitors.

- How to create successful shopping experiences, based on what you learn about customer intention and preference. For example, you might learn that, for customers who entered your site looking for an Android tablet, filtered for memory above 64GB, sorted based on decreasing price and then sorted by highest product review, the most commonly bought tablets were XXX and that certain other tablets were never purchased. You'll see what additional items this type of customer often purchased. Using this knowledge, you can guide look-alike customers to quickly find the item or items that best suit them.

If you ran a small shop and were on a first-name basis with each customer, you would already have such insights and would rely on them to improve your business. In e-commerce, with millions of unseen customers, recapturing this level of insight is extraordinary. We are not talking about invasive spying techniques. You can get valuable insights from studying even anonymous online customer journeys.

Your stores of big data allow you to ask new questions from old data. When you notice a sales spike over the past quarter and wonder how this related to a certain popular item, you can search through detailed historic data to see which customer visits included searches or views of that item. This flexibility in after-the-fact analysis is only possible with big data solutions.

In statistical analysis, as in the Target example, the customer journey data will provide new features for your analytic models. In the past, your models used customer age, income and location, but you can now add search terms and filters, search result orderings and item views. Knowing that a customer bought an unscented hand cream was a signal of possible pregnancy for Target. Knowing that the customer specifically searched for hand cream that is unscented would have been an even stronger signal.

Keep in mind

If your website sees significant customer engagement, you should start using a big data system to store and analyse the detailed online activity. You'll benefit from this analysis even if the visitors remain anonymous.

Your detailed customer journey logs will accumulate at a rate of several gigabytes or even terabytes of unstructured data per day. You won't use your traditional databases for this. We'll talk more about selecting appropriate databases in Chapter 8.

Additional quantities of data

Some analytic models require very little data to work properly. (You need just two points to fit a line.) But many models, especially machine learning models, work much better as they are fed more data. Michele Banko and Eric Brill, researchers at Microsoft in 2001, demonstrated how certain machine learning methods never stopped benefitting from more data, even as they were gorged with extreme amounts.[27] Such machine learning algorithms truly benefit from big data.

The examples above focused heavily on retail applications. I'll round out the chapter with a case study from medical research.

Case study
Cancer research

Big data is playing an increasingly important role in cancer research, both for storing and for analysing important genomic data. There are numerous applications, but I'll briefly mention two: genomic storage and pathway analysis

Every cancer is different, even for patients with the same type of cancer. A single tumour mass may have 100 billion cells, each mutating in a different way, so that studying only a sample of tumour cells will not give the complete picture of what is happening in that individual.

Technology is making it possible for cancer researchers to record the data from more and more of those cancer cells. Since 2003, with the completion of the Human Genome Project, the cost of sequencing genomes has dropped dramatically, as shown in Figure 3.2.

The result is that we are building up a huge catalogue of genomic data, particularly related to cancer. Estimates are that scientists will soon be sequencing and storing more than an **exabyte** of genomic data every year.

Big data technologies are also providing the tools for studying that data. Cancers are characterized by how they disrupt cell protein pathways, and these disruptions differ from patient to patient. To gain deeper insight into these patterns, researchers have developed a method where gene interaction networks are modelled as graphs of 25 thousand vertices and 625 million edges. Protein pathways then correspond to subnetworks in this graph. Researchers can identify connected subnetworks mutated in a significant number of patients using graph

▶

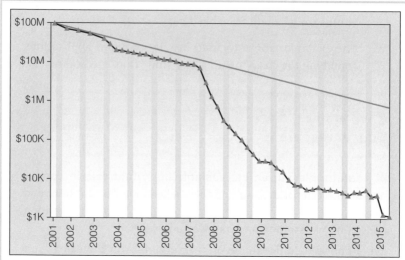

Figure 3.2 Historic cost of sequencing a single human genome.[28,29]

algorithms running on big data technologies (such as **Flink**). Such methods have already brought insights into ovarian cancer, acute myeloid leukaemia and breast cancer.

But not all applications of big data methods to cancer research have been successful, as we'll see in a case study in Chapter 12.

Takeaways

- Big data technologies enable you to bring business value from otherwise unmanageable data.
- Big data technologies allow you to operate in a much more data-driven manner.
- Big data opens the door to new analytic methods and makes traditional methods more accurate and insightful.
- Online customer journey is an example of big data that has proven valuable in many applications.
- Big data has many applications to medical research

Ask yourself

- When was the last time you uncovered an unexpected insight within your data? Do you have people and processes in place to promote data-driven insights?

- Which analytic techniques currently used within your organization could be improved by incorporating new data sources not available when those techniques were first built?

- What problems have you previously written off as 'too difficult to solve' because you didn't have the necessary data or computing power? Which of these might you now be able to solve with big data technologies?

Chapter

Use cases for (big) data analytics

In this chapter, I'll cover important business applications of analytics, highlighting the enhancements of big data technologies, either by providing scalable computing power or through the data itself. It is not uncommon for these applications to raise KPIs by double digits.

A/B testing

In **A/B testing**, also called **split testing**, we test the impact of (typically small) product modifications. We divide customers into random groups and show each a different version. We run the test for a few weeks and then study the impact. Any attribute of your website can be tested in this way: arrangements, colours, fonts, picture sizes, etc. Companies run hundreds of A/B tests over the course of a year to find what best impacts total sales, bounce rate, conversion path length, etc.

A/B testing is the life blood of online companies, allowing them to quickly and easily test ideas and 'fail fast', discarding what doesn't work and finding what does. Beyond simply observing customer behaviour, A/B testing lets you take an active role in creating data and making causal statements. You're not simply watching customers, you're creating new digital products and seeing how the customers react. A/B testing can boost revenue by millions of dollars.

A/B testing is not in itself a big data challenge, but coupling A/B testing with a big data application makes it much more effective. There are several reasons for this.

- By eliminating sampling, big data allows you to perform deep dives into your target KPIs, exploring results within very specific segments. To illustrate with a simplistic example, if you run an A/B test in Europe where the A variant is English text and the B variant is German text, the A variant would probably do better. When you dive deeper, splitting the results by visitor country, you get a truer picture.

  If you run an e-commerce platform with several hundred product categories and customers in several dozen countries, the variants of your A/B test will perform very differently by category and location. If you only study the summary test data, or if you only keep a small percentage of the test data (as was the standard practice in many companies), you'll lose the quantity of data you would need to draw a meaningful conclusion when a product manager asks you about the performance of a certain product in a certain market within a specific time window (for example, when a high-priced marketing campaign was run during a major network event). It is big data that gives you these valuable, detailed insights from A/B tests.

- The second way in which big data improves A/B testing is that, by allowing you to keep all the customer journey data for each testing session, it allows you to go beyond KPIs and begin asking nuanced questions regarding how test variants impacted customer journey. Once you have added a test variant ID to the big data customer journey storage, you can then ask questions such as 'which variant had the shorter average length of path to purchase?' or 'in which variant did the customer purchase the most expensive product viewed?' These detailed questions would not be possible in standard A/B implementations without big data.

- The third way, which we touched on in the last chapter, is that big data lets you answer new questions using data that you've already collected. Conjectures about user responses to product changes can sometimes be answered by looking to vast stores of historical data rather than by running new tests.

To illustrate, imagine a company such as eBay is trying to understand how additional item photos might boost sales. They could test this by listing identical products for sale, differing only in the number of photos, and running this experiment for several weeks. If they instead used a big data system, they could immediately comb through the historical data and identify such pairs of products which had already been sold. Power sellers on a site such as eBay would have already run such selling experiments for their own benefit. eBay need only find these user-run experiments already stored in the big data storage system. In this way, the company gets immediate answers to their question without waiting for new test results.

Recommendation engines/next best offer

Recommendation engines have proven their worth for many companies. Netflix is the poster child for recommendation engines, having grown user base and engagement metrics not only by acquiring and producing video content, but also through personalized recommendations.

In e-commerce, a key tactical capability is to recommend the products at the appropriate moments in a manner that balances a set of sometimes conflicting goals: customer satisfaction, maximum revenue, inventory management, future sales, etc. You must assess which product would most appeal to each customer, balanced against your own business goals, and you must present the product to the customer in a manner most likely to result in a purchase.

If you're a publisher, you are also facing the challenge of recommending articles to your readers, making choices related to content, title, graphics and positioning of articles. Even starting with a specific market segment and category (world news, local news, gardening, property etc.), you need to determine the content and format that will most appeal to your readers.

Case study
Predicting news popularity at The Washington Post[30]

The Washington Post is one of the few news agencies that have excelled in their creation of an online platform. Acquired by Amazon

▶

founder Jeff Bezos in 2013, it's no surprise it has become innovative and data-driven. In fact, Digiday called The Post the most innovative publisher of 2015. By 2016, nearly 100 million global readers were accessing online content each month.

The Post publishes approximately 1000 articles each day. With print, publishers choose content and layout before going to press and have very limited feedback into what works well. Online publishing provides new insights, allowing them to measure readers' interactions with content in real time and respond by immediately updating, modifying or repositioning content. The millions of daily online visits The Post receives generate hundreds of millions of online interactions, which can immediately be used to steer publishing and advertising.

The Post is also using this big data to predict article popularity, allowing editors to promote the most promising articles and enhance quality by adding links and supporting content. Importantly, they can monetize those articles more effectively. If the model predicts an article will not be popular, editors can modify headlines and images to increase success metrics such as views and social shares.

The Post's data-driven culture is paying off. In an age where traditional publishers are struggling to reinvent themselves, The Post recently reported a 46 per cent annual increase in online visitors and a 145 per cent increase in annual digital-only subscriptions.[31]

We see how the move to online provided insight when articles were being read and shared. The publisher could see which articles were clicked (thus demonstrating the power of the headline and photo), which were read to the end (based on scrolls and time on page) and which were shared on social media. This digital feedback enabled a feedback loop not possible in print. However, using the digital feedback effectively requires the publishers to turn to digital data solutions. As the data grows, accelerates and becomes more complex, the publisher needs advanced tools and techniques for digital insights. To illustrate, consider a publisher who knows the number of readers of certain articles, but wants to understand the sentiment of the readers. This publisher might start collecting and analysing text data from mentions of articles on social media, using sentiment analysis and more complex AI techniques to understand an article's reception and impact.

For merchants, recommending grew more difficult. Placing an item for sale online made it easy to sell, but customers became faceless and often anonymous. As a merchant, you need to know what products customers are most likely to buy, and you need to know how to help them. Both require a continuous feedback cycle which is responsive to each question and action of the customer. When the customer enters the store, you form a sales strategy from first impressions. A young girl will likely buy different items than an older man. The first question from the customer will indicate their intention, and their response to the first items they see will give insights into their preferences.

Recommendation engines typically use a blend of two method-ologies. The first, called collaborative filtering, contributes a recommendation score based on past activity. The second, content-based filtering, contributes a score based on properties of the product. As an example, after I've watched *Star Wars* Episode IV, collaborative filtering would suggest *Star Wars* Episode V, since people who liked Episode IV typically like Episode V. Content-based filtering, however, would recommend Episode V because it has many features in common with Episode IV (producer, actors, genre, etc.). An unwatched, newly released movie would not be recommended by the collaborative algorithm but might be by the content-based algorithm.

Big data is what makes recommendation engines work well. If you're building a recommendation engine, you'll want to calibrate it using abundant, detailed data, including browsing data, and this is provided by your big data stores. The big data ecosystem also provides you with the scalable computing power to run the machine learning algorithms behind your recommendation engines, whether they are crunching the numbers in daily **batch jobs** or performing real-time updates.

Your recommendation engine will work best when it can analyse and respond to real-time user behaviour. This ability, at scale, is what the big data ecosystem provides. Your customers are continuously expressing preferences as they type search terms and subsequently select or ignore the results. The best solution is one that learns from these actions in real time.

Forecasting: demand and revenue

If your forecasting model was built without incorporating big data, it probably is a statistical model constructed from a few standard variables and calibrated using basic historic data. You may have built it using features such as geography, date, trends and economic indicators. You may even be using weather forecasts if you are forecasting short-term demand and resulting revenue.

Big data can sharpen your forecasting in a couple of ways.

- First, it gives you more tools for forecasting. You can keep using your standard statistical models, and you can also experiment using a neural network trained on a cluster of cloud-based **graphical processing units (GPUs)** and calibrated using all available data, not just a few pre-selected explanatory variables. Retailers are already using such a method to effectively forecast orders down to the item level.

- Second, big data will provide you with additional explanatory variables for feature engineering in your current forecasting models. For example, in addition to standard features such as date, geography, etc., you can incorporate features derived from big data stores. A basic example would be sales of large ticket items, where increasingly frequent product views would be a strong predictor of an impending sale.

IT cost savings

You can save significant IT costs by moving from proprietary technology to open-source big data technology for your enterprise storage needs. Open-source technologies run on commodity hardware can be 20–30 times cheaper per terabyte than traditional **data warehouses.**[32] In many cases, expensive software licenses can be replaced by adopting open-source technologies. Be aware, though, that you'll also need to consider the people cost involved with any migration.

Marketing

Marketing is one of the first places you should look for applying big data. In Dell's 2015 survey,[1] the top three big data use cases among respondents were all related to marketing. These three were:

1. Better targeting of marketing efforts.
2. Optimization of ad spending.
3. Optimization of social media marketing.

This highlights how important big data is for marketing. Consider the number of potential ad positions in the digital space. It's enormous, as is the number of ways that you can compose (via keyword selection), purchase (typically through some bidding process) and place your digital advertisements. Once your advertisements are placed, you'll collect details of the ad placements and the click responses (often by placing invisible pixels on the web pages, collectively sending millions of messages back to a central repository).

Once customers are engaged with your product, typically by visiting your website or interacting with your mobile application, they start to leave digital trails, which you can digest with traditional web analytics tools or analyse in full detail with a big data tool.

Marketing professionals are traditionally some of the heaviest users of web analytics, which in turn is one of the first points of entry for online companies that choose to store and analyse full customer journey data rather than summarized or sampled web analytics data. Marketing professionals are dependent on the online data to understand the behaviour of customer cohorts brought from various marketing campaigns or keyword searches, to allocate revenue back to various acquisition sources, and to identify the points of the online journey at which customers are prone to drop out of the funnel and abandon the purchase process.

Social media

Social media channels can play an important role in helping you understand customers, particularly in real time. Consider a recent

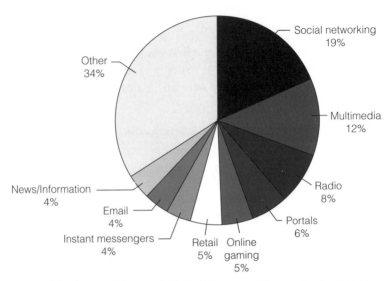

Figure 4.1 Share of the total digital time spent by content category.
Source: comScore Media Metrix Multi-Platform, US, Total Audience, December 2015.[33]

comScore report showing that social networking accounts for nearly one out of five minutes spent online in the US (see Figure 4.1)

Social media gives insight into customer sentiment, keyword usage and campaign effectiveness, and can flag a PR crisis you need to address immediately. Social media data is huge and it moves fast. Consider Twitter, where 6000 tweets are created each second, totalling 200 billion tweets per year.[34] You'll want to consider a range of social channels, as each may play an important role in understanding your customer base, and each has its own mixture of images, links, tags and free text, appealing to slightly different customer segments and enabling different uses.

Pricing

You may be using one or more standard pricing methods in your organization. These methods are specialized to fit specific sectors and applications.

Financial instruments are priced to prevent arbitrage, using formulas or simulations constructed from an underlying mathematical model of market rate movements. Insurance companies use risk- and cost-based models, which may also involve simulations to estimate the impact of unusual events. If you are employing such a simulation-based pricing method, the big data ecosystem provides you with a scalable infrastructure for fast **Monte Carlo simulations** (albeit with issues related to capturing correlations).

If you are in commerce or travel, you may be using methods of dynamic pricing that involve modelling both the supply and the demand curves and then using experimental methods to model price elasticity over those two curves. In this case, big data provides you with the forecasting tools and methods mentioned earlier in this chapter, and you can use the micro-conversions in your customer journey data as additional input for understanding price elasticity.

Customer retention/customer loyalty

Use big data technologies to build customer loyalty in two ways.

First, play defence by monitoring and responding to signals in social media and detecting warning signals based on multiple touch points in the omni-channel experience. I'll illustrate such an omni-channel signal in the coming section on customer churn. In Chapter 6, I'll also discuss an example of customer service initiated by video analysis, which is a specific technique for applying non-traditional data and AI to retain customers and build loyalty.

Second, play offense by optimizing and personalizing the customer experience you provide. Improve your product using A/B testing; build a recommendation engine to enable successful shopping experiences; and deliver customized content for each customer visit (constructed first using offline big data analytics and then implemented using streaming processing for real-time customization).

Cart abandonment (real time)

Roughly 75 per cent of online shopping carts are abandoned.[35] Deploy an AI program that analyses customer behaviour leading up to the point of adding items to shopping carts. When the AI predicts that the customer is likely to not complete the purchase, it should initiate appropriate action to improve the likelihood of purchase.

Conversion rate optimization

Conversion rate optimization (CRO) is the process of presenting your product in a way that maximizes the number of conversions. CRO is a very broad topic and requires a multi-disciplinary approach. It is a mixture of art and science, of psychology and technology. From the technology side, CRO is aided by A/B testing, by relevant recommendations and pricing, by real-time product customization, by cart abandonment technologies, etc.

Product customization (real time)

Adjust the content and format of your website in real time based on what you've learned about the visitor and on the visitor's most recent actions. You'll know general properties of the visitor from past interactions, but you'll know what they are looking for today based on the past few minutes or seconds. You'll need an unsampled customer journey to build your customization algorithms and you'll need streaming data technologies to implement the solution in real time.

Retargeting (real time)

Deploy an AI program to analyse the customer behaviour on your website in real time and estimate the probability the customer will convert during their next visit. Use this information to bid on retargeting slots on other sites that the customer subsequently visits. You should adjust your bidding prices immediately (a fraction of a second) rather than in nightly batches.

Fraud detection (real time)

In addition to your standard approach to fraud detection using manual screening or automated rules-based methods, explore alternative machine learning methods trained on large data sets.[36]

The ability to store massive quantities of time series data provides both a richer training set as well as additional possibilities for features and scalable, real-time deployment using **fast data** methods (Chapter 5).

Churn reduction

You should be actively identifying customers at high risk of becoming disengaged from your product and then work to keep them with you. If you have a paid usage model, you'll focus on customers at risk of cancelling a subscription or disengaging from paid usage. Since the cost of acquiring new customers can be quite high, the return on investment (ROI) on churn reduction can be significant.

There are several analytic models typically used for churn analysis. Some models will estimate the survival rate (longevity) of your customer, while others are designed to produce an estimated likelihood of churn over a period (e.g. the next two months). Churn is typically a rare event, which makes it more difficult for you to calibrate the accuracy of your model and balance between false positives and false negatives. Carefully consider your tolerance for error in either direction, balancing the cost of labelling a customer as a churn potential and wasting money on mitigation efforts vs the cost of not flagging a customer truly at risk of churning and eventually losing the customer.

These traditional churn models take as input all relevant and available features, including subscription data, billing history, and usage patterns. As you increase your data supply, adding customer journey data such as viewings of the Terms and Conditions webpage, online chats with customer support, records of phone calls to customer support, and email exchanges, you can construct a more complete picture of the state of the customer, particularly when you view these events as a sequence (e.g. receipt of a high bill, followed by contact with customer support, followed by viewing cancellation policy online).

In addition to utilizing the additional data and data sources to improve the execution of the traditional models, consider using artificial intelligence models, particularly deep learning, to reduce churn. With deep learning models, you can work from unstructured data sources rather than focusing on pre-selecting features for the churn model.

Predictive maintenance

If your organization spends significant resources monitoring and repairing machinery, you'll want to utilize big data technologies to help with predictive maintenance, both to minimize wear and to avoid unexpected breakdowns. This is an important area for many industries, including logistics, utilities, manufacturing and agriculture, and, for many of them, accurately predicting upcoming machine failures can bring enormous savings. In some airlines, for example, maintenance issues have been estimated to cause approximately half of all technical flight delays. In such cases, gains from predictive maintenance can save tens of millions annually, while providing a strong boost to customer satisfaction.

The Internet of Things (IoT) typically plays a strong role in such applications. As you deploy more sensors and feedback mechanisms within machine parts and systems, you gain access to a richer stream of real-time operational data. Use this not only to ensure reliability but also for tuning system parameters to improve productivity and extend component life.

This streaming big data moves you from model-driven predictive maintenance to data-driven predictive maintenance, in which you continuously respond to real-time data. Whereas previously we may have predicted, detected and diagnosed failures according to a standard schedule, supplemented with whatever data was periodically collected, you should increasingly monitor systems in real time and adjust any task or parameter that might improve the overall efficiency of the system.

Supply chain management

If you're managing a supply chain, you've probably seen the amount of relevant data growing enormously over the past few years. Over half of respondents in a recent survey of supply chain industry leaders[37] indicated they already had or expected to have a petabyte of data within a single database. Supply chain data has become much broader than simply inventory, routes and destinations. It now includes detailed, near-continuous inventory tracking technology at the level of transport, container and individual items, in addition to real-time environmental data from sensors within transports.

These same survey respondents indicated that the increased visibility into the movements of the supply chain was their most valuable application of big data technology, followed by an increased ability to trace the location of products. These were followed by the ability to harvest user sentiment from blogs, ratings, reviews and social media. Additional applications of value included streaming monitoring of sensor readings (particularly for temperature), equipment functionality, and applications related to processing relevant voice, video and warranty data.

Customer lifetime value (CLV)

As you work to understand your marketing ROI and the cost of customer churn, you'll want to analyse customer lifetime value (CLV), the total future value that a customer will bring to your organization. A basic CLV calculation (before discounting) would be

$$\text{(Annual profit from customer)} \times \text{(Expected number of years the customer is active)} - \text{Cost of acquiring customer}$$

Estimating CLV for customer segments lets you better understand the ROI from acquisition efforts in each segment. If the expected profits don't exceed the acquisition costs, you won't want to pursue those customers.

The accuracy of your CLV calculation increases with your ability to sub-segment customers and your ability to compute the corresponding churn rates. Your ability to mitigate churn and to further activate customers through cross-sell, up-sell and additional conversion rate optimization will boost your CLV.

Use available big data to produce the more refined customer segmentation. The additional data will primarily consist of digital activity (including acquisition source, webpage navigation, email open rates, content downloads and activity on social media) but for some industries may also include audio and video data produced by your customer. To illustrate, you may find that customers you acquire from social media referrals will remain with you longer than customers you acquire from price comparison sites.

Lead scoring

Lead scoring is the art/science/random guess whereby you rank your sales prospects in decreasing order of potential value. A 2012 study by Marketing Sherpa reported that only 21 per cent of B2B marketers were already using lead scoring,[38] highlighting abundant room for growth.

Use lead scoring to help your sales team prioritize their efforts, wasting less time on dead-end leads and using their time for high-potential prospects. You'll borrow techniques you used in churn analysis and CLV to generate a lead score, which multiplies the likelihood of lead conversion with the estimated CLV of the lead.

For attempted cross-sell and up-sell to existing customers, start from the same sources of customer data. If the lead is not a current customer and conversions are infrequent, you'll generally have much less data for them, so you'll need to select and calibrate models that work with more limited data (e.g. machine learning models won't generally work).

Consider using AI methods to detect signals in audio and video records matched with sales events. If there is sufficient training data, these methods could be trained to automatically flag your high-potential sales prospects (in real time). We mention a very basic example of such a method in Chapter 6.

Human resources (HR)

If you work in HR, leverage the tools and methods for lead scoring, churn analysis and conversion rate optimization to find and attract the best candidates, reduce employee churn and improve KPIs related to productivity and employee satisfaction.

Recruitment and human resource professionals examine similar data to understand and ultimately influence recruitment success, increase employee productivity and minimize regretted attrition. In addition to traditional HR data (demographics, application date, starting date, positions, salaries, etc.), leverage the new data becoming available to you, such as response patterns for different types of job postings, photos and videos of candidates, free text on CVs / interview notes / emails / manager reviews and any other digital records available, including activity on social media.

Pay attention to privacy laws and to the privacy policies of your organization. The analytics on this data can provide valuable insights even without retaining personally identifiable information. It can be done not only at the level of individual employees but also at progressively aggregate levels: department, region and country.

Sentiment analysis

You can get insights into the intentions, attitudes and emotions of your customers by analysing their text, speech, video and typing rhythms, as well as from data returned by onsite monitors such as video cameras and infra-red monitors.

Always-up monitoring systems can give you public reaction to your marketing or news events. If you are concerned with security or fraud, you can use sentiment analysis to flag high-risk individuals at entrance points or during an application process, forwarding these cases to trained staff for manual evaluation.

As with any AI, sentiment analysis will not be 100 per cent accurate, but it can prove invaluable in bringing trending opinions to your attention much more quickly than manual efforts, and in quickly combing through extensive and rapidly moving data to identify common themes. In addition, some systems can spot features and patterns more accurately than human observers.

> **Keep in mind**
>
> Big data technologies help you do many things better but are not a silver bullet. You should typically build your first solutions using traditional data, and then use big data to build even better solutions.

So far, we've painted the big picture of big data and AI, and we've looked at several business applications. We end Part 1 of this book with a slightly more detailed look at the tools and technologies that make big data solutions possible. We'll then move to Part 2, which focuses on the practical steps you can take to utilize big data within your organization.

Takeaways

- We provide a brief overview of 20 applications of business analytics, some of which are incrementally improved and some significantly improved by big data technologies.

Ask yourself

- Which of these twenty business applications are most important for your organization? For those already in use within your organization, where could you add additional data sources, particularly big data or omni-channel data?
- Which KPIs could significantly improve your results if they increased by 5 per cent? Consider that a concerted analytic effort should increase a well-managed KPI by 5 per cent and a poorly managed KPI by 20 per cent or more.

Chapter

5

Understanding the big data ecosystem

What makes data 'big'?

When referring to data as 'big data', we should expect to have one or more of 'the three Vs' first listed in 2001 by Gartner's Doug Laney: *volume*, *velocity* and *variety*. You might also see creative references to additional Vs, such as *veracity*.[39]

- **Volume** refers to the sheer quantity of data that you store. If you store the names and addresses of your immediate family, that is data. If you store the names and addresses of everyone in your country, that is a lot of data (you might need to use a different program on your computer). If everyone in your country sends you their autobiography, that is big data. You would need to rethink how you store such data.

  I described earlier how the NSA recently completed a data centre that may reach 'one yottabyte' of storage[40] and how YouTube is perhaps the largest non-government consumer of data storage today. This is thanks to over one billion YouTube users,[41] half of whom are watching from mobile devices, and who, all told, are uploading new video content at such a rapid rate that the content uploaded on 15 March alone could include high-definition video of every single second of the life of Julius Caesar. The world continues to change rapidly, and scientists predict that we will soon be storing newly sequenced genomic data at a rate even greater than that of YouTube uploads.[42]

Case study
Genomic data

Biologists may soon become the largest public consumers of data storage. With the cost of sequencing a human genome now under $1000, sequencing speeds at over 10,000 giga base pairs per week, and the creation of over 1000 genomic sequencing centres spread across 50 countries, we are now seeing a doubling of stored genomic data every 7 months.

Researchers at the Simons Center for Quantitative Biology at Cold Spring Harbor Laboratory (CSHL) recently published a paper[42] predicting that the field of genomics will soon become the world's largest consumer of incremental storage. They predict that as many as 2 billion people will have their full genomes sequenced over the next ten years.

In addition, new genome sequencing technologies are revealing previously unimagined levels of genome variation, particularly in cancers, meaning that researchers may eventually sequence and store thousands of genomes per individual.

- **Velocity** refers to how rapidly data accumulates. Processing 100,000 product search requests on your webshop over the course of an hour is very different from processing those requests in a fraction of a second.

  Earlier I introduced the Square Kilometre Array (SKA), a next-generation radio telescope designed to have 50 times the sensitivity and 10,000 times the survey speed of other imaging instruments.[43] Once completed, it will acquire an amazing 750 terabytes of sample image data per second.[44] That data flow would fill the storage of an average laptop 500 times in the time it takes to blink and would be enough to fill every laptop in Paris in the span of a Parisian lunch break. When eBay first purchased its gold-standard, massively parallel database from Teradata in 2002, its storage capacity at that time would have been filled by this SKA data in under two seconds.

Not every velocity challenge is a volume challenge. The SKA astronomers and the particle physicists at CERN discard most data after filtering it.

- **Variety** refers to the type and nature of the data. Your traditional customer data has set fields such as *Name*, *Address* and *Phone Number*, but data is often free text, visual data, sensor data, or some combination of data and time stamps, which together preserve a complex narrative. The systems you use to store and analyse such data need to be flexible enough to accommodate data whose exact form can't be anticipated. We'll talk about technologies that can handle such data in Chapter 8.

The three Vs describe major challenges you'll need to overcome, but they also open tremendous opportunities for you to benefit from data in ways previously not possible.

Keep in mind

As a rule of thumb, 'big data' refers to data challenges that could not be handled in an affordable, scalable way prior to recent developments in how we program 'normal' computers to work in unison.

Distributed data storage

There are three basic ways to deal with storage limitations:

1. Buy a more expensive device with more storage, although twice the storage could mean five times the price. At some point, there is no bigger device available.
2. Buy separate storage devices. In this case, you lose the functionality that comes from having your data in one place.
3. Discard whatever data doesn't fit in your system.

There is a more expensive technique. Specialized vendors produced massively parallel processing (MPP) databases, consisting of special networked hardware working in unison. They could scale up by adding additional machines, but this quickly became very expensive.

As we discussed in Chapter 1, two things changed the economics of data storage:

1. The dramatic fall in the price of commodity computers (general purpose computers from HP, Dell, etc.), so that companies could afford to purchase small armies of them, even hundreds or thousands.

2. The spread of open-source technologies for coordinating such computers, particularly the creation of the Hadoop software framework.[45]

Hadoop made it possible to scale storage costs linearly using the **Hadoop Distributed Files System (HDFS).** You no longer needed to spend five times the money for a bigger machine with twice the storage, but could get twice the storage with two smaller machines or ten thousand times the storage with ten thousand smaller machines. As we'll discuss later, there are now several alternatives to Hadoop's HDFS for low-cost, scalable storage.

The economics of scaling storage changed dramatically and there was a fundamental change in our ability to work with data. The ability to ask new questions of old data that you would otherwise have discarded brings increased agility to your organization. You can analyse any historical event at any level of detail. Rather than solving a storage problem, you can focus on leveraging data for competitive advantage.

Consider that in a 2015 Dell survey,[1] 73 per cent of organizations reported they had big data that could be analysed, with 44 per cent still uncertain how to approach big data. A similar study by Capgemini and EMC highlighted the disruptive nature of big data, with 65 per cent of respondents perceiving they risk becoming irrelevant and/or uncompetitive if they do not embrace big data, 53 per cent expecting to face increased competition from start-ups enabled by data and 24 per cent already experiencing entrance of competitors from adjacent sectors.[32]

Distributed computations

New big data technologies will help you do more than store data. They will help you compute solutions much more quickly. Consider the classic problem of searching for a needle in a haystack. If you split the haystack into 1000 small piles and put 1000 people on the project, your search will go much faster. The bigger the haystack, the more you'll benefit from this approach. Many software applications work like this, and falling hardware prices have made it very attractive to purchase (or rent) additional computers to put to work on your most important problems.

The original Hadoop framework had two core components:

1. HDFS, Hadoop's distributed, scalable file system; and

2. MapReduce, a programming model for running computations across multiple computers.

MapReduce provided a method to spread certain tasks over many machines, much like the haystack illustration. MapReduce did for computations what HDFS did for storage. Computing problems that previously took days could be run in hours or minutes using normal programming languages and hardware.

MapReduce is now being overtaken in many applications by a newer framework called Spark, developed at Berkeley University's AMPLab and released in 2014. Spark has several advantages over MapReduce, including running 100× faster in many applications.

Fast/streaming data

'Fast data' is high-velocity data requiring immediate reaction. Many organizations consider leveraging fast data to be more important than leveraging big data.[32] Much of today's data is both fast and big, and fast data is often seen as a subset of big data.[46]

Consider the benefits of analysing and acting on your data in real time, while also storing it for later use. In the process, you'll want to combine your new streaming data with data you've already stored when making real-time decisions. You'll face special challenges implementing such real-time applications, and you'll want to refer to developments related to the **lambda architecture** and, more recently, Apache **Beam**.

Why is processing streaming big data so challenging? Not only do you need to consider additional requirements in speed, bandwidth, consistency and timing, you often need real-time analytics for real-time responses, such as:

- fraud checks during credit card purchases,
- shutting down a malfunctioning machine,
- rerouting data/traffic/power flow through a network, or
- customizing webpages in real time to maximize the likelihood that a shopper makes a purchase, basing your customization on their last few seconds of activity.

You'll see more streaming data with IoT (Internet of Things) technology, such as from moving vehicles or manufacturing systems. Because you'll have strict **latency** (time) and bandwidth (volume) restrictions in such applications, you'll need to make stricter choices regarding what to process in real time or to store for later analysis. This brings us to the topic of fog computing.

Fog computing/edge computing

Fog computing, also called 'edge computing', is processing data at the edges of a sensor network (see Figure 5.1). Such an architecture alleviates problems related to bandwidth and reliability.

If your sensor networks transfer the collected sensor data to a central computing hub and then return the results for execution, they will typically be limited by the transmission rates of technologies such as LoRaWAN (Long Range Wide Area Network), which is roughly 400 times slower than your phone's 3G cellular network.

Such data movement may be completely unnecessary, and it introduces an additional potential point of failure, hence the push to move computing closer to the edge of the network.

Open-source software

Open-source software is what allowed big data technology to spread so rapidly. It is impossible to talk about big data without making frequent reference to this broad ecosystem of computer code that has been made freely available for use and modification.

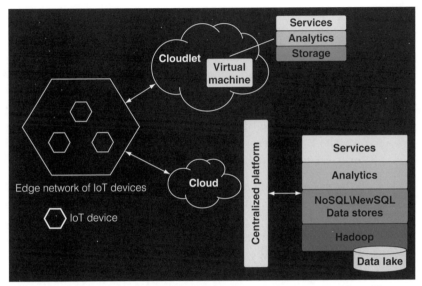

Figure 5.1 Fog computing landscape, image from reference 46, p. 15

History of open-source

In the early days of computing, computer code could be considered an idea or method, preventing it from being protected by copyright. In 1980, copyright law was extended in the USA to include computer programs.[47]

In 1983, Richard Stallman of MIT countered this ruling by establishing a movement aimed at promoting free and open collaboration in software development. He created a project (1983), a manifesto (1985) and a legal framework (1989) for producing software that anyone was free to run, copy, distribute or modify, subject to a few basic conditions (such as not attempting to resell the software). For reasons beyond comprehension, he called this the GNU project[48] and the legal framework was the first of several versions of the General Public License (GPL).

One of the foundational pieces of software released in the GNU project was the now ubiquitous operating system known as Linux, released in 1992. I would be exaggerating only slightly if I said that Linux is now or has at one time been used by just about every software developer on this planet.

The other ubiquitous and functionally foundational piece of software released as open-source in the 1990s was the Apache HTTP server, which played a key role in the growth of the web. This software traces its origins back to a 1993 project involving just eight developers. In the fifteen years after its initial 1995 release, the Apache HTTP server provided the basic server functionality for over 100 million websites.[49]

Whereas most companies built business models around not making their software freely available and certainly not releasing source code, many software developers strongly supported using and contributing to the open-source community. Thus, both proprietary and open-source streams of software development continued to grow in parallel.

Soon something very interesting happened, marking a significant turning point in open-source. In 1998, Netscape Communications Corporation, which had developed a browser competing with Microsoft's Internet Explorer, announced that it was releasing its browser source code to the public.[50] Open-source was now growing from both corporate and private contributions.

In 1999, the originators of the already widely used Apache HTTP server founded the Apache Software Foundation, a decentralized open-source community of developers. The Apache Software Foundation is now the primary venue for releasing open-source big data software. Hadoop was released to Apache in 2006, and much of the software that runs on top of Hadoop's HDFS has been licensed under the terms of the Apache Foundation.

Figure 5.2 shows the growth in Apache contributors 1999–2017.

Licensing

There are several commonly used licenses for open-source software, differing in restrictions on distribution, modification, sublicensing, code linkage, etc. The original GPL from GNU is currently up to version 3. The Apache Foundation has its own version, as do organizations such as MIT.

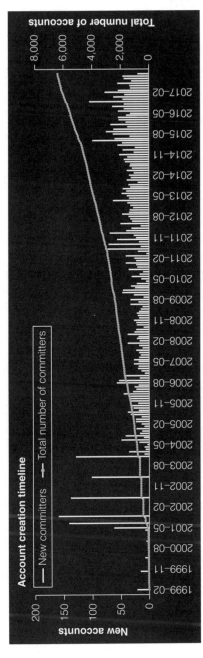

Figure 5.2 Growth in Apache contributors: 1999–2017.[51]

Code distribution

Open-source software is typically made available as source code or compiled code. Changes to code are managed on a **version control system (VCS)** such as Git, hosted on platforms such as GitHub or Bitbucket. These systems provide a transparent way to view each addition or modification in the code, including who made a change and when. Software developers use contributions to such projects as bragging rights on their CVs.

Advantages of open-source

Many programmers contribute to open-source projects out of conviction that software should be free. You might wonder why a corporation would contribute code, giving away software they've spent significant resources on developing. Software companies themselves have wondered this. In 2001, Jim Allchin, at the time a Microsoft executive, was quoted as saying:

> 'I can't imagine something that could be worse than <open-source> for the software business and the intellectual-property business.'[52]

Despite the strength of this statement, Microsoft has since made several contributions to open-source.

There are various reasons you might want to open-source your company's software, including:

- to encourage the spread of software for which you can sell supporting services or enhanced, non-public, versions;
- to encourage the spread of software that will promote your other revenue streams. For example, when you open-source software running on hardware or (paid) software that you produce;

- to harness the collective development power of the open-source community in debugging and improving software you're developing to perform an important task within your company;

- to satisfy licensing requirements when you've incorporated code subject to open-source licensing in a product that you are reselling; and

- to promote your company as technologically advanced and help attract top talent.

Keep in mind

Adding software to open-source repositories is a good way to promote yourself and your company

---

Open-source for big data

Open-source has been instrumental in the big data ecosystem. The concepts behind Hadoop were originally published in a research paper in 2003, and Hadoop itself was created in 2006 as an (open-source) Apache project. Since then, dozens of software tools connected with Hadoop have been created in or moved to the Apache Foundation.

Many big data tools not related to Hadoop are either part of the Apache Foundation or licensed under the Apache Licence. MongoDB and Cassandra are two prominent examples. Spark, the RAM-based big data framework that we mentioned previously, was developed at Berkeley Labs and subsequently released as an Apache project. Neo4j, a graph database for big data, is not Apache but has a community version that is open-sourced, currently under version 3 of GPL.

There are many big data tools, both hardware and software, that are still proprietary, and there are situations in which you might prefer to use these proprietary solutions rather than open-source software. We'll talk more about why in Chapter 9.

Cloud computing

Simply put, cloud computing is a model for sharing centralized computer resources, whether hardware or software. Cloud computing comes in a variety of forms. There are public clouds, such as AWS, Azure and Google Cloud, and there are private clouds, whereby larger corporations maintain centralized computing resources that are allocated in a flexible manner to meet the fluctuating needs of internal business units.

Cloud computing has become ubiquitous, both in personal and business use. We use cloud computing when we use Gmail or allow Apple or Google to store the photos we take on our smartphones. Companies such as Netflix depend heavily on cloud computing to run their services, as do the people using **Salesforce** software.

There are several reasons cloud computing is such a key part of the big data ecosystem.

- **Speed and agility:** Cloud computing makes it fast and easy for you to experiment and scale up your data initiatives. Once an idea is in place, you no longer need to get approval for large hardware purchases, followed by a waiting period for installation. Instead, a credit card and minimal budget can enable you to launch a data initiative within a few minutes.

- **Reduced reliance on specialized skills:** Beyond the basic setup of hardware and networking, which fall under the category of Infrastructure as a Service (IaaS), there are companies that will also provide the software layers necessary to launch a (big) data initiative. These include **Platform as a service (PaaS)**, which encompasses the operating system, databases, etc., and **Software as a Service (SaaS),** which encompasses hosted applications such as Azure ML, Gmail, Salesforce, etc. The greater the number of non-core tasks you can offload to a service provider, the more you can focus on your key differentiators.

- **Cost savings:** Whether cloud computing is cheaper than maintaining hardware and services in-house depends on your use case and on changing market prices. Either way, cloud computing provides you with an opportunity to move IT costs from CapEx to OpEx.

There are several more nuanced factors you should consider with cloud computing, and I'll return to these when I talk about governance and legal compliance in Chapter 11. For now, the most important point is the tremendous gains in agility and scalability that cloud computing provides for your big data projects.

Now that we've described the main topics related to big data, we're ready to talk about how to make it practical for your organization.

Takeaways

- Data solutions today are designed to handle high volume, variety and velocity.
- The key to processing such data is software that distributes the storage and computation loads over many smaller computers.
- Publicly available, open-source software has been invaluable in spreading big data technology.
- Cloud computing is a significant enabler for companies to initiate and scale their data and analytics endeavours.

Ask yourself

- Which software applications do you absolutely need to build in-house or purchase from a vendor rather than leveraging open-source software? For all other applications, what open-source software is available and how might you benefit from it?
- Which of your business applications would benefit from technology allowing you to analyse and provide appropriate responses in real time? Think, for example, of real-time personalization, recommendations, marketing, route planning and system tuning.
- Are important applications in your organization being delayed because you are moving data back and forth to process it centrally? Which of those applications could be accelerated by decentralizing computations or utilizing streaming technologies such as Spark or Flink?

- Which parts of your IT have you not yet moved to the cloud? If you previously thought the cloud to be too risky or too expensive, which of your previous concerns are still relevant today? Cloud technology is developing quickly, and traditionally cautious companies are becoming more open to it.

Part

2

Making the big data ecosystem work for your organization

Chapter

How big data can help guide your strategy

As you evaluate your company's strategy, perhaps even considering a strategic pivot, you'll want to gather and utilize all available data to build a deep understanding of your **customers**, your **competitors**, the **external factors** that impact you and even your **own product**. The big data ecosystem will play an important role in this process, enabling insights and guiding actions in ways not previously possible.

Your customers

Customer data is one of your most important assets. There is more data available today than ever before, and it can tell you much more than you'd expect about your customers and potential customers: who they are, what motivates them, what they prefer and what their habits are. The more data you collect, the more complete your customer picture will become, so make it your goal to collect as much data as possible, from as many sources as possible.

Getting the data

Start by identifying all customer interaction points:

- Visits to your digital platforms: websites, apps and kiosks'.
- Interactions with customer support: phone, email, online chat, etc.
- Social media, including direct messaging, tweets, and posts on accounts you own or they own'.

- Records of physical movement, including store videos and movement logs. There are several technologies for monitoring movement, including embedded sensors, Wi-Fi, Bluetooth, beacons, and even light frequencies in combination with smartphone apps.
- In some industries, you will have access to additional (non-geo) sensor data from sensors, RFID tags, personal fitness trackers, etc., which may provide data such as bio-medical readings, accelerometer data, external temperature, etc.

For each interaction point, make an inventory of:

- what data you can possibly collect;
- what the potential uses of that data are; and
- what privacy and governance factors you should consider (see Chapter 11).

For many organizations, the interaction points will consist of physical and web stores, Apple (iOS) and Android apps, social media channels, and staff servicing customers in stores, call centres, online chat and social media. I'll illustrate with a few examples.

Digital

Start with your digital platforms. First the basics (not big data yet).

You'll probably already have some web analytics tags on your website that record high-level events. Make sure you also record the key moments in the customer journey, such as when the visitor does an onsite search, selects filters, visits specific pages, downloads material, watches your videos or places items in the checkout basket. Record mouse events, such as scrolls and hovers. Make sure these moments are tagged in a way that preserves the details you'll need later, such as adding the details of product category, price range, and product ID to the web tags associated with each item description page. This will allow you to quickly do top-of-mind analysis, such as identifying how often products in certain categories were viewed, or how effective a marketing campaign was in driving a desired event. In the end, you'll probably have several dozen or even several hundred specific dimensions that you add to your out-of-the-box web analytics data. This isn't yet big data.

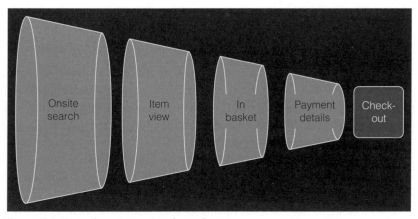

Figure 6.1 Sample conversion funnel.

With the additional detailed tags that you've implemented, you'll be able to analyse and understand many aspects of the customer journey, giving insights into how different types of customers interact with the products you've presented them. We'll show examples of this below.

If you haven't already done so, set up conversion funnels for sequential events that lead to important conversion events, such as purchases. Figure 6.1 shows how a basic purchase funnel might look.

Each intermediate goal in the conversion funnel is a micro-conversion, together leading to a macro-conversion ('checkout' in this case). Choose your micro-conversions in a way that reflects increasing engagement and increased likelihood of a final conversion. The funnels you set up will enable you to analyse drop-off rates at each stage, allowing you to address potential problem points and increase the percentage of visitors progressing along each stage of the funnel, eventually reaching the conversion event at the end of the funnel. Depending on your product, customer movement down the funnel may span several days, weeks or months, so you'll need to decide what to consider 'drop-off'.

For privacy and governance in your website, research and comply with local laws governing the use of web cookies. Make a list of where you are storing the browsing data that identifies the individual user (such as IP address) and how you later use the insights you've gathered in customizing your interactions with each user.

For example, if you personalize your content and marketing based on the users' online actions, you'll need to consider the ethical and legal implications. Remember the example from Target.

Now the big data part. You've set up the web analytics to record details most meaningful for you. Now hook your web page up to a big data system that will record every online event for every web visitor. You'll need a big data storage system, such as HDFS, and you'll need to implement code (typically JavaScript) that sends the events to that storage. If you want a minimum-pain solution, use Google Analytics' premium service (GA360), and activate the BigQuery integration. This will send your web data to Google's cloud storage, allowing you to analyse it in detail within a few hours. If you need data in real time, you can change the GA Java-Script method sendHitTask and send the same data to both Google and to your own storage system. Such an architecture is illustrated below in Figure 6.2. Note that Google's terms and conditions require that you not send **personally identifiable information (PII)** (we'll discuss PII further in Chapter 11).

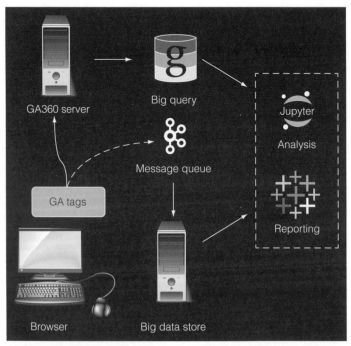

Figure 6.2 Example architecture for a streaming big data implementation.
Source: icons from BigQuery, Apache Kafka, Jupyter notebooks and Tableau.

You'll now have the raw customer (big) data you need to formulate a very detailed understanding of your customers, as described later in this chapter.

Customer support

Consider recording and analysing all interactions with sales agents and customer support: phone calls, online chats, emails and even videos of customers in stores. Most of this data is easy to review in pieces, but difficult to analyse at scale without advanced tools. As you store these interactions, your customer support agents should enrich them with additional information, such as customer ID and time of day', and label them with meaningful categories, such as 'order enquiry', 'new purchase', 'cancellation' or 'complaint.' You can then save the entire data file in a big data storage system (such as MongoDB or HDFS). We'll show valuable ways to use this data later in this chapter.

Physical movements

You have a choice of several technologies for monitoring how your customers are moving within your stores. In addition to traditional video cameras and break-beam lasers across entrances, there are technologies that track the movement of smartphones based on cellular, Bluetooth or Wi-Fi interactions. Specialized firms such as ShopperTrak and Walkbase work in these areas. Such monitoring will help you understand the browsing patterns of your customers, such as what categories are considered by the same customers and how much time is spent before a purchase decision. It will help you direct your register and support staff where needed. Again, this data is valuable even if the customer is kept anonymous.

When a customer arrives at the register and makes a purchase, possibly with a card that is linked to that customer, you will be able to see not only what is being purchased, but also what other areas of the store were browsed. You might use this information in future marketing or you might use it to redesign your store layout if you realize that the current layout is hampering cross-sell opportunities.

These are just a few examples. In general, start collecting and storing as much detail as possible, making sure to consider business value, to respect customer privacy and to comply with local laws in your collection, storage and use of this data. Be careful not to cross the line between 'helpful' and 'creepy'. Keep your customers' best interests in mind and assume any techniques you use will become public knowledge.

Keep in mind

Try to provide a useful service to your customer for each piece of privacy you ask them to sacrifice. For example, if your smartphone app tracks a customer's physical location, make sure the customer gets valuable location-based services from this app. Also, provide a better, personalized online experience to visitors who are logged in to your website. In this way, your interests are aligned with those of your customers.

Linking customer data

Link the customer data from your interaction points to give a holistic picture of customer journey. If a customer phones your call centre after looking online at your cancellation policy webpage, you should be able to connect those two events in your system. To do this, enter a unique customer field (such as phone number or user name) along with the call record.

If you are monitoring a customer walking through your store, link that footpath with subsequent register sales information (subject to privacy considerations). Do this by recording the timestamp and location of the point of sale with the footpath data. Combine the data centrally to give the complete picture.

Sometimes you'll use anonymous customer data, such as when analysing traffic flow. Other times you'll use named-customer data, such as when analysing lifetime activity. For the named-customer applications, you'll want to de-duplicate customers. This is difficult, and you'll probably have limited success. The best situation is when customers always present a unique customer ID when using your service. In an online setting, this would require a highly persistent and unique login (as with Facebook). Offline, it typically requires photo ID. In most situations, you won't have this luxury, so use best efforts to link customer interactions.

You'll typically face the following problems in identifying your customers:

- **Problem:** Customers will not identify themselves (e.g. not logging in).
- **Possible solutions:** Use web cookies and IP addresses to link visits from the same visitors, producing a holistic picture of anonymous customer journeys extended across sessions. Use payment details to link purchases to customers. Smartphones may provide information to installed apps that allow additional linking. Talk to your app developers about this.
- **Problem:** Customers create multiple logins.
- **Possible solutions:** Clean your customer database by finding accounts that share key fields: name, email address, home address, date of birth, or IP address. A graph database such as Neo4J can help in this process, as illustrated in Figure 6.3. Work with the business to create logic for which customers to merge and which to associate using a special database field (e.g. 'spouse of'). Change your account creation process to detect and circumvent creation of duplicate accounts, such as by flagging email addresses from existing accounts.

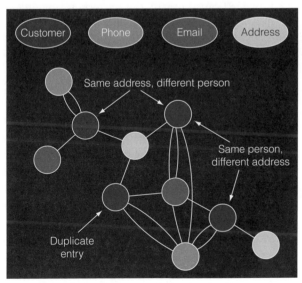

Figure 6.3 A graph database can help de-duplicate customers.

Using the data

Much of your customer data will be useful even in the aggregate and anonymized format provided by your standard web analytics tool. You'll see how many customers came at any hour of the day as well as useful information such as average time spent onsite, number of pages viewed, how many entered at each page or from each marketing campaign, etc. You'll also see the total transactions made by customer segments, such as geography and acquisition source. This will give you a picture of how and when your products are being used, particularly when matched against marketing campaigns, holidays, service downtimes and new initiatives.

Customer journey

The big data insights get much more useful when you use data to build an understanding of the intents, preferences and habits of your customers. You should already be segmenting your customers into **personas** based on static features such as home address, gender, language, age and possibly income level. Note that Google Analytics can provide useful demographic information (from their DoubleClick cookie) if you enable this functionality.

Broaden your segmentation criteria to include customer journey data, such as those listed below.

- **What filters do they most often use? Is it Price high-to-low? Price low-to-high? Highest rated item? Newest product?** Customers sorting price low-to-high are probably price conscious. Those sorting price high-to-low or by highest rating are probably quality conscious. Those sorting newest first may be quality conscious or perhaps technophiles or early adopters. Those sorting by rating may be late adopters or quality conscious. All of this will impact how you interact with them. If a customer is quality conscious but not price conscious, you should present them with high-quality products in search results and marketing emails, and you should not be presenting them with clearance sales of entry-level products. You'll want to interact with the price-conscious customer segments in exactly the opposite way.

- **How many items do they typically consider before making a purchase?** This information will help you decide when to intervene in the shopping process, such as by offering a discount when a customer is about to leave without making a purchase.

- **What categories do they visit most often?** This will help you segment the customer and return the most relevant results for ambiguous search phrases (such as 'jaguar' the car vs 'jaguar' the animal or Panama City, Florida vs Panama City, Panama). You'll also use this information to guide which items you market to the customer.

- **Do they change the shipping option to save fees?** Again, a signal of price-conscious customers.

- **Do they read customer reviews? Do they write reviews?** If they always read reviews, don't present them with poorly reviewed items in your marketing emails, search results, or cross-sell frames. If they often write reviews, or if they own social media accounts with an unusually high number of followers, make sure they get 'golden glove' customer support.

- **What types of marketing do they best respond to? Do they open newsletters? Do they respond to flash sales?** Don't fill their inbox with marketing they never respond to. Give them the most relevant media and you'll increase the odds they respond rather than clicking 'unsubscribe'.

- **If they are active on social media, what are the topics and hashtags they most frequently mention? Can you use this knowledge to market more effectively to them?** Here again, you are building customer personas with all relevant information. Try to get connected to their social media accounts. As we mentioned in Chapter 4, what they do here can tell you a lot about them.

Customer segments (personas)

Using data you've collected, decide what factors are most meaningful in dividing your customers into segments (personas). Examples would be 'price-sensitive males aged 20 to 30' or perhaps 'high-spending technophiles who make quick purchasing decisions', or 'customers who browse daily across specific categories but buy only on discount'. You can construct these segments in a qualitative way, using the intuition of marketing experts guided by the data, or you can construct the segments in a quantitative way, using analytic tools such as **clustering** and **principal component analysis.** Both are valid methods, but if you have a lot of data that can be segmented in many ways, the quantitative approach will probably be more effective.

Inventory

This customer journey data will give deeper insights into how your inventory impacts customer experience. As you consider removing items with low sales, the customer journey data may show a high percentage of profitable transactions by customers who found your site searching for those non-profitable products. You'll want to understand more about the customer journey of those customers, what they looked for and why they made their decisions, before you make the decision to remove products which may have attracted those customers to your shop in the first place.

On the other hand, you may be selling a product that is often showing up in online search results but is of no interest to your customers, as demonstrated by your customer journey data. In this case, you should either change the display of the product search result, or remove the item altogether, as it is taking up valuable search real estate.

Critical intervention

Apply both basic analysis and advanced machine learning to your customer data and you'll likely find ways to decrease churn and increase sales. Basic analysis of where and when your customers are active will help you with scheduling the shifts and skill sets of your support personnel. It will also signal what the customer is likely to do next (a customer visiting your appliance store twice last week may be preparing for a significant purchase).

With a bit more analysis, you'll start detecting subtle but important signals. A European telecommunications company recently analysed data on customers cancelling their subscriptions and found that a large number followed the same three or four steps prior to cancellation, such as reviewing their contract online, then phoning customer support, then disputing a bill in person and then cancelling the contract. By linking those events, the company identified signals of impending churn so it could take action.

At an even more advanced level, machine learning techniques could detect pending account cancellation or the likelihood of a sale based on an analysis of text, audio or video. Such a system might be a significant investment of your time and resources, but you might have the business case to justify it, or you might find a vendor who has already developed a technology suitable for your application, as illustrated in the next case study.

Case study
Actionable customer insights from in-store video feeds

The *Economist* magazine recently wrote about two innovations in the use of video analysis. Realeyes, an emotion-detection firm based in London, found that shoppers who entered a store smiling spent a third more than others. In another pilot programme, a European bookstore chain began using software from Angus.ai to monitor when its customers walked to the end of an aisle and returned with a frown. The software then discretely messaged a sales clerk to help. The result was a 10 per cent rise in sales.[53]

As always, consult your company's privacy officer to stay within the limits of the law, stay aligned with your customers' best interests and don't do anything that would give negative publicity if it were made public.

Your competitors

It's especially challenging to get good information about your competitors. Information brokers such as Nielsen, Comscore and SimilarWeb will sell their estimations of traffic to your competitors' sites and apps, possibly including referrer information. The website trends.google.com gives charts for the number of searches for specific terms, which in turn give indications of how you compare with your competitors for brand search (see Figure 6.4).

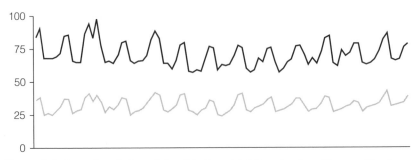

Figure 6.4 Searches in Brazil for 'McDonalds' (top line) vs 'Burger King' (bottom line) Q2, 2017 (Google Trends).

You'll be able to get information on competitor inventory, services and physical locations by scraping websites. Your technology team can help with this (you can use a tool such as Selenium). If you are competing on price, you'll want to adjust your pricing based on your competition's proximity to your customers. For physical locations, that will be based on address and transportation routes. For online sales, that will be partially influenced by the referrer sending a visitor to your site. Customers arriving from price comparison sites should be considered price-conscious and at high risk of buying from your competitors.

Work to increase your share of wallet, the percentage of a customer's spend that goes to your business rather than to competitors'. Start by using the detailed customer data you have collected and see what categories and what specific products are typically purchased by the same customer segments. You'll be able to see which customers are already making those cross-purchases, which are browsing but not purchasing, and which are active in only one category.

Identify the products your customers are purchasing elsewhere to see where you are losing share of wallet. If you sell groceries and your customer only buys fruits and vegetables, you'll know they are buying milk and eggs elsewhere. If you sell electronics and they only buy smartphones, you'll know they are buying computers elsewhere. This will help identify areas where you need to compete harder. By using the customer segments you've created, you'll see if your competition is appealing more to quality-conscious customers, marketing-reactive customers, high-spenders, etc.

Monitor online job boards to get insights into competitors' initiatives. A significant increase in postings for a location or job function will indicate activity in that area. Create watch lists of competitor employees' LinkedIn profiles and monitor them for anomalies in profile updates. If an unusually high number of employees are updating their LinkedIn profiles, it may signal turmoil or pending layoffs within the company. Similarly, natural language processing run on company public statements can uncover unusual activity. This technique has been used effectively to signal pending initial public offerings.

External factors

Your strategy will be influenced by factors ranging from government regulation to local weather. If you are in the travel and tourism industry, regional holidays will impact long-range bookings and weather will influence impulse bookings. The price of commodities will influence production and transport costs, and exchange rates or political turmoil will influence cross-border activity.

Much of the impact of external factors will be from traditional (small) data, but newer (big) data sources will provide additional, valuable signals. Keep an eye on changes in online customer activity, which may signal unexpected factors requiring your attention. To illustrate, consider how Google Maps and Waze can detect construction or road closures simply by studying driver movements.

To give another example, you may not be aware of the release of an innovative new product until you see it in onsite searches or detect the impact in sales of your other products. If you are running a hotel chain and have a property in Scranton, Pennsylvania, you may have no idea there is a major convention about an obscure topic being planned there during the second week in February. If you are prepared with a forecast of booking rates for February, you'll see the unexpected spike in the customer activity in your booking site and call centres already in October, before you even know about the February conference. By monitoring customer activity, you can act to raise room rates in October before running out of underpriced February inventory a few weeks later.

To this end, you should construct regular forecasts of key metrics, including number of visits and sales projections. You'll do this by consulting historic figures, projecting growth rates, and speaking with your business units to consider anything out of the ordinary (holiday cycles, major events, regulatory or economic changes, etc.). These forecasts should be segmented down to the levels at which you can steer your operations (such as product and region) and should preferably be made at daily granularity. If you automatically monitor these figures at daily or weekly granularities you can raise an alert whenever they move above or below expected levels, signalling when some external factor is impacting your business in an unexpected way.

Your own product

You need to truly understand your own service and product offerings when evaluating your strategy. You may not understand them as well as you think, and your customers may perceive them in completely different ways than you'd expect. What is working and what is not working? How are customers responding to your products? Where are you losing money through inefficiencies?

If your web offering is a significant part of your business, find out what is working there and work to make it better. Create and track micro-conversions to see how your items are performing even before a purchase is made. These provide valuable insights even if they are not part of a funnel analysis.

Track the customer engagement with your other digital offerings.

- What is the **applause rate** on your social media? (How many times are your tweets liked or retweeted? How many comments on your Facebook posts?)
- How many people download your material?
- How many people sign up for your newsletter?

Test changes in your products by running A/B tests, which you'll do in the following way:

1. Propose one small change that you think may improve your offering. Change one frame, one phrase, or one banner. Check with your development team to make sure it's an easy change.

2. Decide what key performance indicators (**KPI**) you most want to increase: revenue, purchases, up-sells, time onsite, etc. Monitor the impact on other KPIs.

3. Run the original and the changed version (A and B) simultaneously. For websites, use an A/B tool such as Optimizely. View the results using the tool or place the test version ID in web tags and analyse specifics of each version, such as by comparing lengths of path to conversion.

4. Check if results are statistically significant using a two-sample hypothesis test. Have an analyst do this or use an on-line calculator such as https://abtestguide.com/calc/.

5. Use your big data system for deeper analysis:

   a. Were there significant changes in customer journey, such as number of categories viewed or filters selected?

   b. Are there key product or customer segments you should manage differently?

   c. Did specific external events influence results?

   d. Did KPIs move in different directions?

Align your assumptions about your product with these new insights. For example:

- Are you trying to compete on price, while most of your revenue is coming from customers who are quality conscious?

- Are you not taking time to curate customer reviews, while most of your customers are actively sorting on and reading those reviews?

If your assumptions about your product don't align with what you learn about your customers' preferences and habits, it may be time for a strategic pivot.

Use modern data and data science (analytics) to get the insights you'll need to determine and refine your strategy. Selectively choose the areas in which you should focus your efforts in (big) data and data science and then determine the necessary tools, teams and processes.

In the next chapter, I'll talk about how to choose and prioritize your data efforts.

Takeaways

- Big data sources will help inform your strategy by giving new insights into your customers, competition, business environment and product.

- There are many new sources of non-traditional data. Take an inventory of what is available and what is most useful.

- You will typically have difficulty linking your customer actions across different touch points.

- Your website and other digital portals can provide detailed information about customer intentions, preferences and habits, signalling when you need to make a tactical change or a strategic pivot.

- Running your A/B tests in combination with a big data system allows you to gather much deeper insights.

Ask yourself

- Make a list of your customer touchpoints. For each, note if you are digitalizing and storing none, some, or all the available data. Rate each touchpoint from 1 to 10 in terms of (a) the value of the data and (b) how difficult it would be to store and analyse additional data from that touchpoint. Multiply those two scores together. The touchpoints with the highest resulting numbers are your most promising new sources of customer data.

- What data sources would you need to link to get a full view of your customer interactions? Is there anything preventing you from linking this data?

- What are ways in which your customers differ in their preferences and behaviour and which might impact the way in which you relate to them and the products and experiences you offer to them?

- What have been the most successful product changes that you made after testing the results of different possibilities?

- Which external data is relevant for your organization: economic data, weather, holiday schedules, etc.?

- Which data sources could give you more insight into your competition? Think of private and public information providers as well as graphs and signals provided by internet companies such as Google and LinkedIn.

Chapter 7

'. . . let's seek to understand how the new generation
of technology companies are doing what they do,
what the broader consequences are for businesses
and the economy . . .' —*Marc Andreessen.*[54]

Forming your strategy for big data and data science

It's exciting for me to sit with business leaders to explore ways in which data and analytics can solve their challenges and open new possibilities. From my experience, there are different paths that lead a company to the point where they are ready to take a significant step forward in their use of data and analytics.

Companies that have always operated with a minimal use of data may have been suddenly blindsided by a crisis or may be growing exasperated by:

- lagged or inaccurate reporting;
- wasted marketing spend;
- time lost to poor sales leads;
- wasted inventory; or
- any one of a host of operational handicaps that can result when data is ignored or data solutions are constructed in a short-sighted manner.

They end up forced to run damage control in these areas, but are ultimately seeking to improve operations at a fundamental level and lay the groundwork for future growth.

Companies that have been operating with a data-driven mindset may be exploring innovative ways to grow their use of data and analytics. They are looking for new data sources and technologies that will give competitive advantages or are exploring ways to quickly scale up and optimize a proven product by applying advances in parallel computing, artificial intelligence and machine learning.

Regardless of which description best fits your company, the first step you'll want to take when re-evaluating your use of data and analytics is to form a strong programme team.

The programme team

Your data initiative programme team should include individuals representing four key areas of expertise:

1. strategic,
2. business,
3. analytic; and
4. technical.

Strategic expertise

You'll need to include someone on the team who has a deep understanding of your corporate strategy. The strategic vision will form the basis for all plans and discussions within the company, including the data strategy. This vision will have been specified by the shareholders, refined by the board of directors, and shaped by the culture within your organization. It will dictate the purpose and principles that underpin how you use data. If your new data strategy is not aligned with the company's overall strategy, your subsequent efforts will not support parallel initiatives within your organization and will fail from lack of internal support.

There are many excellent frameworks for developing corporate strategies, and I won't explore those but rather emphasize the importance of synchronizing data and corporate strategies. I'll illustrate with the framework of Tracey and Wiersema,[55] in which the strategic focus of a corporation may be to develop an advantage in exactly one of the following sectors: customer intimacy, product leadership or operational excellence. Within this strategic framework, if your company has chosen to differentiate itself through enjoyable shopping and excellent customer service (e.g. customer intimacy) you'll choose a data strategy leading to improved customer experience (e.g. an intelligent personalization engine) rather than one focusing on cutting operational costs.

Business expertise

According to a recent global study, business teams lead the adoption of big data more frequently than IT teams.[56] Big data is a team sport, and your efforts will likely fail without strong input and support from your non-technical colleagues. If they aren't convinced of the benefits of your data initiatives, you are probably doing something wrong.

Harvest the intuition of colleagues with the deepest understanding of the customer, the product and the market. Get them involved at the start of your analytics programme and keep them closely involved at each stage of development.

You'll see many advantages from involving business stakeholders in the initial stages.

- They will understand the nuances of the market, including the impact of demographics, product segments, and seasonality/holidays.
- They will have a good idea what is most important to customers and what customers view as your product differentiators. They will have spoken with a variety of customers over the years. The insights they've gained will be invaluable to your analytics programme.
- They will remember past initiatives your company and similar companies have tried. They will remember what did or didn't work well. They will tell you why things went wrong and suggest how they could go better next time.
- They will have insights into other companies in your industry, perhaps having worked there, and will be familiar with their strengths, weaknesses and key differentiators.
- They will tell you 'obvious' details that can easily save you months of effort.

Incorporating business intuition is a tricky balancing game, and I've seen it go both ways. I've seen analysts sitting in isolation come up with models that completely missed key aspects of the business, and I've seen business directors make strong statements later proven by the data to be completely wrong.

Intuition sometimes is right and sometimes not, so it's important to take seriously any non-measurable input from the business, while subsequently seeking data to verify that intuition.

Involve the business experts in the following ways:

1. To introduce the basics of how the business operates, including the customer base, the products and the competitors. They should explain the competitive differentiators of each market player, how companies and their market share have been changing over time, and how customers themselves have changed during this period.

2. To explain their insights into the business, in areas such as customer preferences, marketing channel effectiveness, customer segment price sensitivity, purchasing rhythms, potential product improvements, etc. They may consider their insights as facts or as hunches. Either way, take them with a grain of salt and use them as starting points until you have had a good look at supporting data. These insights will form the basis for your initial list of analytics projects, either as assumptions to be verified or as opportunities for further analysis, leading ultimately to product improvements.

3. To provide continuous feedback during the data collection and modelling processes. The business experts will typically have some of the best insights into which data is reliable and which data should be disregarded. These insights will be critical for analysts. In addition, the business experts will have intuition into which data is most relevant for specific analysis.

Let your business stakeholders review your analytic models. They can often quickly catch errors in a modelling process by flagging aspects that seem counter-intuitive.

To illustrate, consider a recent study at the University of Washington. Researchers took a standard data set and created a classification model that performed with an accuracy of 57 per cent (rather weak). A modelling expert then removed spurious (misleading) data and improved the accuracy to 70 per cent. The researchers gave the same data set to non-technical model reviewers and asked them to also remove the spurious features from the data. After three such iterations, the non-technical reviewers had beaten the technical modeller in identifying the most relevant data, improving the accuracy of the final model from 57 per cent to over 75 per cent,[57] and thus demonstrating the value of having non-technical business experts review analytic models.

4. To provide the broader context of product history and what has brought you to where you are now. This gives you context and helps you avoid repeating costly mistakes. It also helps you to understand the accumulated learning and the thought processes that form the history of your company. It can resurrect options previously dismissed but which have since become more attractive, perhaps due to advances in technology, market movements or customer base.

It is important to rehash options over time. Not only is technology developing rapidly, but people are also changing in how they use technology. As an example, we have as consumers developed over the last fifteen years an increased willingness to enter credit card details and a decreased responsiveness to certain forms of marketing.

Your company may have developed a whole product strategy based on customer insights that are no longer relevant. By understanding the historic backdrop that led you to where you are today, your project team will be better positioned to consider which questions need new answers and which improvements might be made through applications of data and analytics.

Analytic expertise

Don't start an analytic initiative without including someone with a strong background in developing and deploying analytic models. I know this sounds obvious, but I've seen large companies try to do just that, and it's painful to watch. You need to include an expert who understands what is possible with data and analytics and can estimate what is needed to attain what is possible. This person should have a strong technical background, several years of analytic leadership experience within a comparable industry setting and a broad understanding of the models, tools and applications available for bringing business value from data and analytics. You can substitute academic experience for industry experience, at a risk.

Your company needs to identify high-potential analytic applications, and it needs to choose from a broad selection of analytic methods and models. In addition to the methods of artificial intelligence and deep learning, which are currently trending, many traditional methods rooted in the fields of statistics, network/graph algorithms, simulations, constrained optimization and data mining have proven their worth over recent decades. Each algorithm has strengths and weaknesses, and you must take care to choose algorithms suited to your data and applications. Considering only a subset of these tools when approaching a business problem will limit your success and can lead to a tremendous waste of effort.

You'll need to understand what techniques will continue to work well as your problem size grows. Each algorithm will differ in how it scales, so your analytics expert should understand whether a technique that performs well with a small data set is likely to scale well to a much larger data set. In summary, it is important to bring a broad understanding of analytic models to the project team.

Keep in mind

You'll need a broad understanding of programming languages and analytic tools, not only the most recently trending technologies, but also a strong understanding of traditional methods.

The tools you'll consider range from basic to advanced functionality. At the most foundational level, there are many programming languages that can be used for building solutions from the ground up. These include Java, C++, Python, SAS, R, S-plus and a host of others, some of which are free and some of which are proprietary. Each programming language will have its own strengths and weaknesses, some of the most important considerations are:

- execution speed;
- ease of development (including the availability of relevant libraries);

- the ability of the language to easily interface with relevant technologies (third party and those of the company itself); and

- the breadth of the user / support base (again including support within the company itself).

You should also be familiar with the development frameworks available for optimizing development and deployment of your base code, and how you can deploy custom code within larger software packages you may use, such as R or Python code within an SAS application.

Overall, you'll need to make a nuanced version of the classic 'build vs buy' decision, deciding how to mix and match pre-existing analytic tools that have differing levels of complexity and inter-operability. Some of these tools will be open-source and some will be proprietary. For some well-established analytic models that have had time to be highly optimized by specialist vendors, such as linear programming, there are strong advantages to investing in an off-the-shelf solution. For specialized AI methods with limited but important application within your business, consider a pay-per-use model from vendors such as Google or Salesforce (Einstein) rather than expending internal effort.

The analytics specialist should bring a broad understanding of potential applications for data and analytics within your organization, along the lines of the applications I've listed in Chapter 4.

As you think about how to utilize data science within your organization, consider:

1. With which analytic applications are the business units already familiar? Web developers may be familiar with A/B testing, finance professionals with statistical forecasting, marketing professionals with funnel analysis and bid optimization, etc.

2. Are there additional best practice analytic applications that the company has not yet considered?

3. Have there been recent technical developments that could improve performance of analytic applications already implemented, such as the incorporation of new big data technologies, algorithms or data sources?

4. Are there innovative methods that have recently been employed in other industries, which may in turn introduce possibilities for new competitive advantages within your industry?

For each of the above points, your analytics specialist should be able to estimate the data, technology and personnel requirements necessary both for prototyping as well as for deployment.

As part of this process, they should be forming a holistic picture of the company's existing and potential data assets, including standard operational, customer and financial data; the raw data collected in data lakes; third-party data that could be purchased or collected; and possibly even the **dark data** within your systems.

Technical expertise

The project team will need technical expertise to ensure operational success. This will be someone with an understanding of the technology for data collection and transfer, general infrastructure and corporate databases. Data is a critical component of analytics initiatives, so your technical expert should bring an understanding of the extent and accuracy of the various data stores within the organization.

Your company may also have one or more operational data stores, data marts and/or data warehouses, which will provide the data for analytics projects. In addition, analysts will need to create tables, sometimes large tables, in one or more of these databases and may even need additional types of databases, such as graph or document databases (discussed further in Chapter 8).

The technical expert will provide direction and assistance related to your computing infrastructure, whether it be in-house server capacity or possibilities to provision in the cloud.

It's important to build solutions that you can maintain long term. This will help you maximize the chance your analytics projects will bring long-term value. Your technical expert will help ensure these projects can integrate with existing technology.

To this end, ask the input of your technology expert regarding:

- acceptable choice of development language, frameworks and operating system;

- requirements for version control and documentation; and
- requirements and resources for testing (QA) and deployment to production.

Your analytics efforts depend on IT support. Many projects fail because they do not get the buy-in of IT. Involving IT from the start serves four purposes.

1. It informs the analytics expert of the available technology landscape.
2. It helps ensure long-term success in the organization by showing what standards and technologies should be utilized.
3. It allows IT to contribute valuable ideas and insights.
4. It helps secure buy-in from IT from the very beginning.

After years of being awoken at 3 am or phoned during a holiday to fix malfunctioning production code, many IT staff will be extremely sensitive to analytics initiatives with even the slightest risk of breaking existing code. They may also be averse to any vagueness or uncertainty in project planning, wanting every project step to be laid out at the start. As we'll see later, analytics projects don't typically lend themselves well to extensive preplanning, so some tension can easily develop in this regard.

Other IT staff can be very eager to try new technologies and new analytic methods. These are typically the younger ones with fewer 3 am experiences under their belts, but sometimes also the senior staff. Quite often, the developers in IT are extremely enthusiastic about analytic projects. These people will typically be some of the strongest and most valuable supporters of your analytics initiatives.

Keep in mind

Your IT professionals may have two goals: stability and/or innovation. Many measure the success of IT in terms of reliability. Others measure its success in terms of creativity and innovation, even if the new features aren't perfect.

The kick-off meeting

Once you've selected your programme team, plan a programme kick-off meeting to lay the strategic foundation for the analytics initiative, sketching the framework for business applications, brainstorming ideas, and assigning follow-on steps, which will themselves lead to initial scoping efforts. The four skill sets represented in the programme team should all be present if possible, although the business expert may cover the strategic input and it is also possible (but not ideal) to postpone technology input until the scoping stage.

Also helpful at this stage is to have detailed financial statements at hand. These figures will help focus the discussion on areas with the most influence on your financials. Bring your standard reports and dashboards, particularly those that include your key performance indicators (KPIs).

Strategic input

Start the kick-off meeting by reviewing the purpose and principles that govern your efforts. Continue by reviewing the strategic goals of the company, distinguishing between the long- and short-term strategic goals. Since some analytics projects will take significant time to develop and deploy, it's important to distinguish the timelines of the strategic goals. If there is no executive or strategic stakeholder involved in the process, the team members present should have access to documentation detailing corporate strategy. If there is no such strategic documentation (as is, sadly, sometimes the case), continue the brainstorming using an assumed strategy of plucking low-hanging fruit with low initial investment, low likelihood of internal resistance and relatively high ROI.

Business input

After reviewing the principles and strategy, review the KPIs used within the organization. In addition to the standard financial KPIs, a company may track any number of metrics. Marketing will track click-through rate, customer lifetime value, conversion rates, organic traffic, etc. Human resources may track attrition rates, acceptance rates, absenteeism, tenure, regretted attrition, etc. Finance will typically track financial lead indicators, often related to traffic (visits, visitors, searches) as well as third-party data.

At this stage, probe more deeply into why certain KPIs are important and highlight the KPIs that tie in most closely with your strategic and financial goals. Identify which KPIs you should most focus on improving.

The business experts should then describe known pain points within the organization. These could come from within any department and could be strategic, such as limited insight into competition or customer segments; tactical, such as difficulty setting optimal product prices, integrating data from recent acquisitions or allocating marketing spend; or operational, such as high fraud rates or slow delivery times.

Ask the business experts to describe where they would like to be in three years. They may be able to describe this in terms of data and analytics, or they may simply describe this in terms of envisioned product offerings and business results. A part of this vision should be features and capabilities of competitors that they would like to see incorporated into their offerings.

Analytics input

By now your business objectives, principles, and strategic goals should be completely laid out (and ideally written up in common view for discussion). At this point, your analytics expert should work through the list and identify which of those business objectives can be matched to standard analytic tools or models that may bring business value in relieving a pain point, raising a KPI, or providing an innovative improvement. It's beneficial to have cross-industry insight into how companies in other industries have benefited from similar analytic projects.

To illustrate this process, a statistical model may be proposed to solve forecasting inaccuracy, a graph-based recommendation engine may be proposed to increase conversion rates or shorten purchase-path length, a natural language processing tool may provide near-real-time social media analysis to measure sentiment following a major advertising campaign, or a streaming analytics framework combined with a statistical or machine learning tool may be used for real-time customer analytics related to fraud prevention, mitigation of cart abandonment, etc.

Technical input

If IT is represented in your kick-off meeting, they will be contributing throughout the discussion, highlighting technical limitations and opportunities. They should be particularly involved during the analytics phase, providing the initial data input and taking responsibility for eventual deployment of analytics solutions. If your technical experts are not present during the initial project kick-off, you'll need a second meeting to verify feasibility and get their buy-in.

Output of the kick-off

The first output of your programme kick-off should be a document that I refer to as *Impact Areas for Analytics*, consisting of the table illustrated in Figure 7.1. The first column in this table should be business goals written in terminology understandable to everyone. The next column is the corresponding analytic project, along the lines of the applications listed in Chapter 4. The next three columns contain the data, technology and staffing needed to execute the project. If possible, divide the table into the strategic focus areas most relevant to your company.

By the end of your kick-off meeting, you should have filled out the first two columns of this matrix.

	Business goals	Analytic projects	Data	Technology	Staffing
First focus area					
Second focus area					
Third focus area					

Figure 7.1 Template for *Impact Areas for Analytics* document.

The second document you'll create in the kick-off will be an *Analytics Effort* document. For each analytics project listed in the first document, this second document will describe:

1. The development effort required. This should be given in very broad terms (small, medium, large, XL or XXL, with those terms defined however you'd like).
2. An estimate of the priority and/or ROI.
3. The individuals in the company who:

   a. can authorize the project; and
   b. can provide the detailed subject-matter expertise needed for implementation. We are looking here for individuals to speak with, not to carry out the project.

   These are the 'A' and the 'C' in the **RASCI** model used in some organizations.

Distribute the meeting notes to the programme team members, soliciting and incorporating their feedback. When this is done, return to the programme sponsor to discuss the *Impact Areas for Analytics* document. Work with the programme sponsor to prioritize the projects, referencing the *Analytics Effort* document and taking into consideration the company's strategic priorities, financial landscape, room for capital expenditure and head-count growth, risk appetite and the various dynamics that may operate on personal or departmental levels.

Scoping phase

Once the projects have been discussed and prioritized with the programme sponsor, you should communicate with the corresponding authorizers (from the *Analytics Effort* document) to set up short (30–60 min) scoping meetings between the analytics expert and the subject matter expert(s). The exact methods and lines of communication and authorization will differ by company and by culture.

During the scoping meetings, speak with the individuals who best understand the data and the business challenge. Your goal at this stage is to develop a detailed understanding of the background and current challenges of the business as well as the relevant data and systems currently in use.

The subject experts and the analytics expert then discuss:

- the proposed analytics solution;
- what data might be used;
- how the model might be built and run; and
- how the results should be delivered to the end user (including frequency, format and technology).

After each scoping meeting, the analytics expert should update the corresponding project entry on the *Analytics Effort* document and add a proposed **minimum viable product (MVP)** to the project description.

The MVP is the smallest functional deliverable that can demonstrate the feasibility and usefulness of the analytics project. It should initially have very limited functionality and generally will use only a small portion of the available data. Collecting and cleaning your full data set can be a major undertaking, so focus in your MVP on a set of data that is readily available and reasonably reliable, such as data over a limited period for one geography or product.

The description should briefly describe the inputs, methodology and outputs of the MVP, the criteria for evaluating the MVP, and the resources required to complete the MVP (typically this is only the staff time required, but it might entail additional computing costs and/or third-party resources). Utilizing cloud resources should eliminate the need for hardware purchases for an MVP, and trial software licenses should substitute for licensing costs at this stage.

Feed this MVP into whichever project management framework you use in your company (e.g. scrum or Kanban). Evaluate the results of the MVP to determine the next steps for that analytics project. You may move the project through several phases before you finally deploy it. These phases might include:

1. several iterations on the MVP to converge on the desired result;
2. further manual application with limited scope;
3. documented and repeatable application;

4. deployed and governed application; and

5. deployed, governed and optimized application

with each successive stage requiring incremental budgeting of time, resources and technology.

It's very important to keep in mind that analytic applications are often a form of Research & Development (R&D). Not all good ideas will work. Sometimes this is due to insufficient or poor-quality data, sometimes there is simply too much noise in the data, or the process that we are examining does not lend itself to standard models. This is why it's so important to start with MVPs, to fail fast, to keep in close contact with business experts and to find projects that produce quick wins. We'll talk more about this in the next chapter when we talk about agile analytics.

Keep in mind

Not all good ideas will work. Start small, get continual feedback, and focus on projects with quick wins.

Case study
Order forecasting for a German online retailer

The Otto group, a German retail conglomerate, employs over 54,000 employees operating in more than 20 countries.[58] Since its establishment in 1949, it has grown to become one of world's largest online retailers. The Otto group has developed several internal applications of AI, one of which nicely illustrates the benefits of close cooperation between business and analytics teams.

At a business level, Otto realized they were losing millions of euros annually because of the costs associated with product returns. The business and analytics teams worked together to address this problem in two phases.

▶

The first phase was to analyse product return data to see what insights emerged. The analysis revealed that a significant portion of returns were products that took more than two days to arrive. Customers left waiting would either purchase the item elsewhere (perhaps at a local shop at discount) or lose enthusiasm for the product. The result was a lost sale and sunk shipping costs. Otto did not itself stock many of the products that it offered, hence the shipping delays.

This data insight led to the second phase of the analytics solution. If Otto could accurately forecast the product orders, it could itself order the inventory even before the customer placed the order. This would allow them to deliver within a shorter time window, resulting in fewer returns. For the analysis, Otto used several billion past transactions, combined with several hundred potentially influential factors (including past sales, online customer journey and weather data).

At this point, the analytics team had a choice of several analytic tools and models. They could have used a classic rule-based approach or a statistical model, selecting and refining features to construct forecasts for product groups. They also considered feeding big data into a deep-learning algorithm.

In the end, they utilized deep-learning technology and what they eventually produced was an analytic tool that could forecast 30-day sales with 90 per cent accuracy. This system now automatically purchases several hundred thousand items per month from third-party brands with no human intervention. Thanks to this analytic project, Otto's surplus stock holding declined by one fifth and their product returns decreased by more than two million items per year.[59]

We see in this example how the Otto group used data and analytics in two key ways in addressing the problem of item returns. The first way was to diagnose the source of the problem, the second was to create a tool they could deploy operationally. These are two of the four primary uses of analytics within organizations. We'll discuss all four in the next chapter.

Takeaways

- Start your analytics programme by forming a programme team with expertise in strategy, business, analytics and technology.
- Identify business objectives and match them with analytic projects, data, technology and staffing.
- Make sure you get sufficient stakeholder input and buy-in at each stage of the programme.
- Start with small projects with low risk and high ROI.

Ask yourself

- If you were to form a programme team with knowledge of strategy, business, analytics and technology, who would be in that team? Ideally you would have one senior person for each of the four areas, but you may need more people to cover the range of important sub-domains.
- Who are the individuals with the best insight into your business, including knowledge of customers, competitors and the history of the industry? These people should at some point have worked directly with your customers.
- What recent events in your organization make this a difficult or a very promising time to initiate new analytics efforts? Who would be the biggest champions and challengers of such an effort?

Chapter 8

'The formulation of a problem is often more essential than its solution . . . To raise new questions, new possibilities, to regard old problems from a new angle requires creative imagination and marks real advances in science.' —*Albert Einstein in* The Evolution of Physics

Implementing data science – analytics, algorithms and machine learning

Four types of analytics

It's quite possible that your biggest initial wins will be from very basic applications of analytics. Analytics can be extremely complex, but it can also be very simple, and the most basic of applications are sometimes the most valuable. The preliminary tasks of collecting and merging data from multiple sources, cleaning the data and summarizing the results in a well-designed table or graph can produce substantial business value, eliminating fatal misconceptions and clearly highlighting performance metrics, costs, trends and opportunities.

Gartner has developed a useful framework for classifying application areas of analytics (shown below). Their *Analytics Ascendancy Model* (Figure 8.1) divides analytic efforts into four categories:

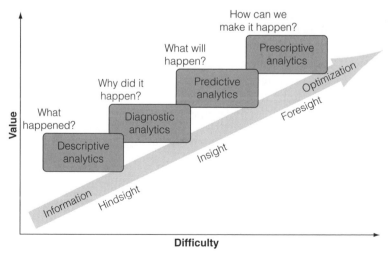

Figure 8.1 Gartner's Analytics Ascendancy Model.

descriptive, diagnostic, predictive and prescriptive. I find this model to be quite useful in discussing analytics.

Descriptive analytics

As you consider your pain points and work to raise KPIs and to reach your strategic goals, many of the issues that surface will be as simple as 'We don't know X about our customers' (behaviour, demographics, lifetime value, etc.) or 'We don't know X about ourselves' (costs, inventory movements, marketing effectiveness, etc.). Getting data-driven answers to such factual questions is what we call 'descriptive analytics'. It is the process of collecting, cleaning and presenting data to get immediate insights.

You'll look to descriptive analytics for three applications:

- **Operational requirements.** Each of your departments will need data to operate effectively. Your finance team, in particular, cannot function without regular, accurate, and consolidated figures. This is why companies often place their **business intelligence** (BI) teams within the finance division.

- **Data insights.** Put as much data as possible into the hands of decision makers. You may choose to have your data (BI) teams situated close to your strategy team and have analysts embedded within your various business units (more on this in Chapter 10).

- **Damage control.** If you've been operating without visibility into your data, you may be blindsided by a drop in one or more KPIs. You need to quickly determine what happened and do damage control. The less data-driven your company, the more likely it is that the crisis will be directly related to profit or revenue (else you would have detected a change in lead indicators). You'll first need to make up ground in descriptive analytics, then move quickly to diagnostic analytics.

To do descriptive analytics well, you'll need the following:

- Specially designed databases for archiving and analysing the data. These databases are most generally referred to as **data warehouses**, although you may use similar technologies with other names.

- A tool for constructing and delivering regular reports and dashboards. Very small companies start with a tool such as MS Excel, but most should be using a dedicated BI tool.

- A system that allows your business users to do **self-service analytics**. They should be able to access data tables and create their own pivot tables and charts. This greatly accelerates the process of data discovery within your organization. To implement a self-service system, you'll need to establish additional data access and governance policies (see Chapter 11).

Diagnostic analytics

Diagnostic analytics are the problem-solving efforts, typically ad hoc, that bring significant value and often require only minimal technical skills (typically some **standard query language (SQL)** and basic statistics). The diagnostic effort consists largely of bringing together potentially relevant source data and teasing out insights either by creating graphs that visually illuminate non-obvious trends or through feature engineering (creating new data fields from your existing data, such as calculating 'time since last purchase' using your customer sales records).

A well-designed graph can be surprisingly useful in providing immediate insights. Consider the graphs presented in Figure 8.2 from Stephen Few's book.[60] Start by looking at the simple data table below to see if any insights or trends stand out.

Job satisfaction by income, education and age				
	College degrees		**No college degrees**	
Income	**Under 50**	**50+**	**Under 50**	**50+**
Up to $50k	643	793	590	724
Over $50k	735	928	863	662

Now consider two different charts constructed from these same eight data points:

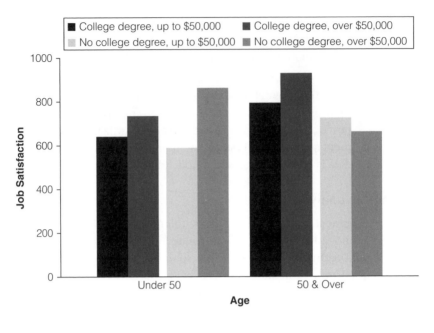

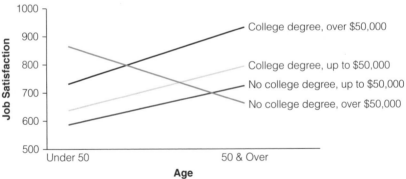

Figure 8.2 Employee job satisfaction.[60]

Notice that the second graph immediately provides a visual insight which does not stand out from the bar chart or the data table: that job satisfaction decreases with age in only one category.

Visuals are powerful tools for diagnostic analytics, and they demonstrate how analytics can be both an art and a science. You'll need creativity and visualization skills to discover and communicate insights through well-designed tables and graphs. As we'll discuss more in Chapter 10, it's important to have someone on your analytics team who is trained in designing graphs and dashboards that can bring your analysis to life.

Predictive analytics

Predictive analytics help you understand the likelihood of future events, such as providing revenue forecasts or the likelihood of credit default.

The border between diagnostic analytics and predictive analytics is somewhat vague, and it is here that we see techniques that require more advanced analytics. Consider customer segmentation, in which an organization divides its customer base into a relatively small number of segments (personas), allowing them to customize marketing and products.

Your initial segments probably used customer demographics (age, gender, location, income bracket, etc.), but you should also incorporate more refined data, such as expressed preferences and habits. RFM (Recency, Frequency, Monetary) is an example of a traditional customer segmentation approach based on purchase history, but the data that informs today's segmentations should include big data: online journey, and sometimes audio and visual data. To form these advanced segments, you'll bring in a lot of data and should use specialized statistical and algorithmic skills (such as principal component analysis, support vector machines, clustering methods, neural networks, etc.)

You'll be able to do much more powerful analysis in predictive analytics. You may be predicting events several years in the future, such as credit default; several weeks or months in the future, when forecasting revenue, supply or demand; several days in the future, when forecasting product returns or hardware failures; or even just a moment in the future, when predicting cart abandonment or the likely response to a real-time advertisement.

The abilities to accurately forecast supply and demand, credit default, system failure or customer response can each have significant impact on your top and bottom lines. They can greatly increase customer satisfaction by enabling adequate inventory levels, relevant advertising, minimal system failures and low likelihood of product return.

Prescriptive analytics

Prescriptive analytics tell you what should be done. Think here of optimal pricing, product recommendations, minimizing churn (including cart abandonment), fraud detection, minimizing operational costs (travel time, personnel scheduling, material waste, component degradation), inventory management, real-time bid optimization, etc.

You'll often use these four analytic layers in succession to reach a goal. For example:

1. descriptive analytics would flag a revenue shortfall;
2. diagnostic analytics might reveal that it was caused by a shortage of key inventory;
3. predictive analytics could forecast future supply and demand; and
4. prescriptive analytics could optimize pricing, based on the balance of supply and demand, as well as on the price elasticity of the customer base.

> **Keep in mind**
>
> You can realize tremendous value simply by organizing your data and making it available across the organization. More advanced projects can come later.

Models, algorithms and black boxes

As you move into more advanced analytics, you'll need to choose analytic models. **Models** are sets of formulas that approximately describe events and interactions around us. We apply models using **algorithms**, which are sequences of actions that we instruct a computer to follow, like a recipe. As you employ an analytic model to solve your business problem (such as predicting customer churn or recommending a product), you'll need to follow three steps:

1. Design the model;
2. Fit the model to the data (also known as 'training' or 'calibrating' the model); and
3. Deploy the model.

Designing the model

Your business problems can typically be modelled in multiple ways. You'll find examples of ways your application has traditionally been modelled in textbooks or online, but you may also experiment with applying models in creative ways. A description of the various models is beyond the scope of this book, but to get a quick overview of commonly used analytic models, pull up the documentation of a well-developed analytic tool such as Rapid-Miner, KNIME or SAS Enterprise Miner, or check out the analytics libraries of the programming languages Python or R. These won't provide exhaustive lists of models, but they will give a very good start. You will be more likely to find a broader range of (academic) algorithms in the R language but you may need to use Python for the cutting-edge big data applications. More on this later.

When speaking about models, we sometimes use the term *model transparency* to indicate the ease with which a model can be explained and understood intuitively, particularly for a non-technical audience. An example of a transparent model would be one that computes insurance risk based on age and geography, and that is calibrated using historical insurance claims. It's easy to understand the factors that influence such insurance premiums. A model that is completely non-transparent is called a **black-box model**, because the end user will not be able to understand its inner workings.

Choose simple, intuitive models whenever possible. A simple model, such as a basic statistical model, is easier to develop, to fit to the data, and to explain to end users than is a more complicated model, such as non-linear support vector machines or neural networks. In addition, transparent models allow end users to apply intuition and suggest modelling improvements, as we saw previously in the University of Washington study, where model improvements suggested by non-technical staff raised accuracy by nearly 50 per cent.

Model transparency is particularly important for applications where outcomes must be explained to healthcare patients, government regulators or customers (e.g. rejection of a loan application).

Black box models from big data

In our daily lives, we draw certain conclusions from concrete facts and others from intuition, an invaluable skill, which is nearly impossible to explain. A thermometer gives a clear indication of fever, but we can simply look at someone we know and perceive when they aren't feeling well. Through years of experience looking at many healthy people and sick people, combined with our knowledge of what this person typically looks like, we 'just know' that the person is not feeling well. Remarkably, models such as neural networks work in a very similar way, trained by millions of sample data points to recognize patterns. Big data enables much stronger computer 'intuition' by providing a massive training set for such machine learning models.

These models, which improve by consuming masses of training data, have recently become significantly better than any transparent algorithm for certain applications. This makes us increasingly dependent on black-box models. Even for classic business applications such as churn prediction and lead scoring, for which we already have reasonably effective and transparent models, data scientists are increasingly testing the effectiveness of black-box models, particularly neural networks (deep learning).

Although an ML method such as neural networks can recognize patterns through extensive training, it is not able to 'explain' its pattern recognition skills. When such a model wrongly labels a dog as an ostrich (as illustrated in Chapter 2), it is very difficult to detect and explain what went wrong.

This lack of transparency is a significant problem in areas such as insurance, law enforcement and medicine. Consider an article published in *Science* magazine in April 2017,[61] describing recent results in the prediction of cardiovascular disease (heart attacks, strokes, etc.). Currently, many doctors evaluate patient risk in this area using eight risk factors, including age, cholesterol level and blood pressure. Researchers at the University of Nottingham recently trained a neural network to detect cardiovascular events, using as inputs the medical records of nearly 400,000 patients. Their model achieved both a higher detection rate (+7.6 per cent) and a lower false alarm rate (–1.6 per cent) than the conventional eight-factor method.

Such a model can potentially save millions of lives every year, but being a neural network it is a black box and hence raises several concerns.

- If patients ask the reason why they were labelled as high risk, the black-box model will not provide an answer. The patients will have difficulty knowing how to reduce their risk.

- If insurance companies use this more accurate method to calculate insurance premiums, they will be unable to justify premiums. At this point, we also start to run into legal implications, as some countries are introducing so-called 'right to explanation' legislation, mandating that customers be given insight into the decision processes that impact them.

There has been recent progress in adding transparency to black box models. The University of Washington has recently developed a tool they call **LIME** – Local Interpretable Model-Agnostic Explanations, which they describe as 'an algorithm that can explain the predictions of any classifier or regressor in a faithful way, by approximating it locally with an interpretable model.'[62] Their tool works by fitting local linear approximations, which are easy to understand, and it can be used for any model with a scoring function (including neural networks).

Fitting the model to the data

After a trained analyst has selected a model (or several candidate models), they'll fit the model to your data, which involves:

1. choosing the exact structure of the model; and
2. calibrating the parameters of the model.

Choosing the structure of the model involves deciding which features in your data are most important. You'll need to decide how to create binned categories (where numbers are grouped into ranges) and whether an engineered feature such as 'average purchase price' or 'days since last purchase' should be included. You might start with hundreds of potential features but use only a half dozen in your final model.

When using neural networks (including deep learning), you won't need to walk through this variable selection or feature engineering process, but you will need to find a network architecture that works for your problem (some sample architectures are illustrated in Chapter 2). You'll follow a trial-and-error approach to choosing the types and arrangements of nodes and layers within the network.

As you calibrate the model parameters, you'll tune the structured model to best fit the training data. Each model will have one or more associated algorithms for adjusting parameters to maximize some target score, which itself describes how well the model fits the training data. Take care to avoid over-fitting the training data, by using a method called **cross-validation** or by assessing a **goodness-of-fit test**.

During the modelling process, try several possible model structures or architectures, using specialized tools and programs to optimize the parameters for each. Assess the effectiveness of each structure or architecture and select one that seems best.

Deploying the model

Develop your models in a programming language and environment suitable for rapid prototyping, using a limited and cleaned data set. Bring in more data after you've demonstrated the effectiveness of the model. Don't spend time making it fast and efficient until it's proven its worth, perhaps even after it has already been deployed in a limited capacity to production.

Many data scientists prototype in the Python or R languages, testing on laptops or a company server. When the code is ready to be deployed to production, you may want to completely re-write it in a language such as C++ or Java and deploy it to a different production system. You'll connect it to production data systems, requiring additional safeguards and governance.

Work with your IT department in selecting:

- hardware for deployment, including memory and processor (typically central processing unit (CPU), but GPU or **tensor processing unit (TPU)** for neural networks);
- architecture that will satisfy requirements for speed and fault-tolerance;
- choice of programming language and/or third-party tool (such as SAS or SPSS);
- scheduling of the computational workload, such as whether it should be run centrally or locally, possibly even at the point of data input (recall our discussion of **fog computing** in Chapter 5).

Work with IT to cover the normal operational processes: backups, software updates, performance monitoring, etc.

Work with your company's privacy officer to make sure you are satisfying requirements for data governance, security and privacy. Your model may be accessing a database with personal information even though the model results do not themselves contain personal information, and this may put you at risk. A government regulation such as Europe's **General Data Protection Regulation (GDPR)** may allow use of personal data for one analytic purpose but not for another, depending on the permissions granted by each individual. I'll talk more about this in Chapter 11, when I discuss governance and legal compliance.

Artificial intelligence and machine learning

I introduced the concepts and recent developments within artificial intelligence in Chapter 2. I'll approach the topic from a more practical angle in this section, putting AI into context within the broader set of analytic tools. Recall that **deep learning** is a form of **neural networks,** reflecting the fact that we now have the technology to run networks with many more layers, hence 'deep'. When I use the term artificial neural networks (ANNs), I'm including deep learning.

You've probably noticed that much of the recent focus within AI has been on ANNs, which are doing a great job solving several classes of problems. But don't expect ANNs to be the best or even a suitable alternative for all problems. They have the advantage of working in domain-agnostic contexts, but if you have specific domain knowledge to bring to bear on your problems, you can incorporate that knowledge in the construction of a more transparent and often more accurate model. In addition, the black-box nature of ANNs generally dictates that you avoid using them except in cases where they provide a clear advantage over more transparent models.

ANNs are especially effective for problems with very large data sets and in which the complexity of the data makes it difficult to apply domain knowledge in your model. Problems involving images are prime candidates for ANNs. Problems involving large amounts of unstructured data with hundreds of features, particularly text, are also good candidates, as ANNs do not require the feature engineering of traditional machine learning techniques. ANNs can work well for natural language processing, but are not always better than alternative methods (such as information retrieval combined with XGBoost).[63] Problems with few features and relatively small amounts of data are generally not good candidates for ANNs.

Dozens of network architectures have been developed,[64] with perhaps the most important being convolutional neural networks (CNNs) and recurrent neural networks (RNNs). Some models use a hybrid mix of architectures. CNNs are particularly useful for image and video analysis and were also used by AlphaGo. RNNs work well with sequential data, such as EEGs and text.

Although building an ANN lets you save effort in structuring your data and engineering features, you'll need to select a network architecture and then train the model. **Model training** is an iterative process of adjusting the model parameters to optimize the accuracy of the model against the available data (the **training data**), which itself must be labelled to enable the training process. This training process is probably the most complex part of utilizing the ANN.

It's becoming much easier to write code to build and deploy ANNs. Google has recently open-sourced TensorFlow, their internal machine learning library for developing and deploying ANNs (as well as other ML applications). TensorFlow is one of several such libraries automating the work required to build, train, and deploy models to various target platforms. Your choice of deployment platform for your ANN is important, since they run much faster on certain types of processors.

You can utilize additional software tools to speed the development process. The Python library Keras, for example, can operate on top of TensorFlow.

AI models such as ANNs are not silver bullets and are still only one part of a larger analytic toolkit. AlphaGo beat the world champion at Go by combining neural networks with the Monte Carlo simulation methods traditionally used for Go.[65] When Apple added deep learning technology to their Siri AI in the summer of 2014, they retained some of their previous analytic models to work alongside it.[66]

Keep in mind

AI models such as deep learning are not silver bullets and are still only one part of a larger analytic toolkit. Don't rush onto the AI bandwagon until you've considered the business benefits and alternative solutions.

In considering what analytic tools to use in your business and whether you should use AI or ML, start by considering the models with proven value for your business problem, taking into consideration available data and resources as well as model complexity, transparency and accuracy.

You can often match your specific business challenges to common classes of data science applications, each of which will have an associated set of algorithms with strong track records of success in addressing those challenges. For example, if you are optimizing personnel schedules, you'll typically use a technique called integer programming; if you are pricing financial instruments, you'll solve financial equations or run Monte Carlo simulations; but if you are building customer segments, you may choose from several viable models, such as logistic regression, support vector machines, decision trees, or a host of other available algorithms, including neural networks.

What remains even with these advances in hardware and software tools are the human resources needed to implement such applications. According to Gartner, there were 41,000 open deep-learning positions at the beginning of 2017, an astounding number when you consider that there were almost no such positions in 2014.[67] Thus, the opportunities afforded by integrating recent advances in neural networks into business applications will continue to add strain to your ability to build data science teams that can cover the increasingly broad span of relevant analytic skills. I'll return to this topic in Chapter 10, when I talk about building an analytics team.

Analytic software

Databases

As you become more ambitious in the types and quantities of data you use, you'll need to look beyond traditional methods of storing and retrieving data. Recent innovations in non-traditional databases for diverse data types form a fundamental component of the big data ecosystem. These databases are often referred to as **noSQL databases**, an acronym for 'not only SQL', since data can be retrieved from them in ways beyond the Standard Query Language (SQL). A key feature typifying these new databases is that the structure (the schema) can be defined on the fly, so we call them 'schema-less databases' and talk about 'schema-on-read'. They are typically designed for efficient horizontal scaling, so we can grow their capacity with additional, rather than more expensive, machines.

You'll need to choose the traditional and non-traditional databases that are most helpful for your applications. I'll now briefly review some of the primary types of databases within the big data ecosystem. To give an idea of the extent of industry activity around each database type, I'll add in parentheses the category ranking scores from db-engines.com as at July 2017.[68]

Relational databases (80 per cent)

These have been the standard databases for operational use for the past 30–40 years. They sit within a relational database management system (RDMS) and consist of individual tables containing data rows with pre-determined columns, such as first name, last name, customer ID, phone number, etc. The tables are related when they share columns with the same information. For example, if there is a customer ID column in both the customer details table and the sales table, then you can compute sales grouped by customer postal code when you cross-reference the two tables. The same relational database can be designed for operational use or designed for use in analytics and reporting (as a data warehouse).

Document-oriented databases (7 per cent)

These are designed for large-scale storage and retrieval of documents, typically containing data stored in flexible **XML** or **JSON** formats. The most commonly used document-oriented database is MongoDB, which is open-source. Document-oriented databases serve well as gateway noSQL solutions, since they can quickly provide general functionality.

Search engine databases (4 per cent)

These are used to power onsite search on many websites, returning search results over vast amounts of inventory using customizable logic to match results to user search queries. With such fundamental functionality, they are often the first foray of websites into the big data ecosystem and are designed to address both the velocity and the variety challenges of big data, particularly for search. These databases are sometimes used for general data storage and analysis, although care should be taken here. Some of the most commonly used search engine databases are Elasticsearch, Solr and Splunk.

Key-value stores (3 per cent)

Entries in these databases are simply key-value pairs. They can get many simple results very quickly, which is particularly useful for online, customer-facing applications. Key-value stores address the velocity challenge of big data.

Wide column stores (3 per cent)

Similar to relational databases in functionality, but providing the flexibility to add data fields on the fly, wide column stores address the variety challenge of big data. For example, a relational database might have 20 pre-defined customer data columns, whereas a wide column store would allow on-the-fly creation of any column type for any customer. If you started a new initiative after several years, such as a premium membership class, you could simply add the required additional columns, such as membership number or total membership points, to a selection of customer records. The data rows for non-members would not change.

Graph databases (1 per cent)

These databases store data in the structure of a graph (a network of nodes and edges). They allow you to query data based on attributes and relationships. For example, you could easily find all of a customer's third-degree connections with a given postal code and membership status. Graph databases take advantage of sparsity and structural features to enable very fast execution of queries that would involve tragically slow multiple inner joins on a traditional relational database. In Chapter 6, we saw an example of using a graph database to de-duplicate customers.

Choosing a database

You may be overwhelmed by the several hundred databases available in the market today. When selecting a database appropriate to your use case, consider not only the type and the cost of the database, but also its place within your current **technology stack**, the breadth of its adoption within the industry (which impacts staffing, maintenance and future capabilities), its scalability, **concurrency** and the tradeoff between consistency, availability and partition tolerance (according to Brewster's CAP theorem, proven in 2002, any database can have at most two of these three). Some of these factors may be critical for your application, while others may be less important.

You can find an ordered list of the currently popular databases for different categories at db-engines.com, which also shows recent trends (see Figure 8.3). At the time of writing, time series databases have been gaining interest faster over the past 12 months than any other type of database (possibly due to their use in IoT), but they are still very much overshadowed by the other types mentioned above. The market research and advisory firms **Gartner** and **Forrester** regularly publish detailed analysis of the databases offered by many larger vendors in their publications known as **Gartner Magic Quadrants** and **Forrester Waves.**

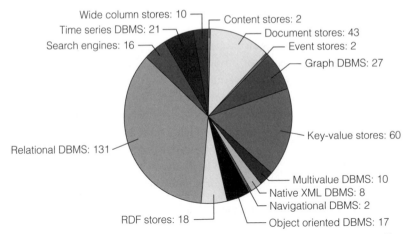

Figure 8.3 Number of listed database systems per category, July 2017.[68]

Programming languages

When developing your analytic models, choose a programming language that fits within your broader IT organization, has well-developed analytics libraries, and integrates well with other data and analytic tools you are likely to use. There is no single best language for analytics, but the top two contenders in online forums are R and Python, at least for the initial stages of development.

In addition to personal preferences, check constraints of the IT environment in which you are working and of third-party software you might use. For example, Python is typically one of the first languages supported by open-sourced big data projects (as was the case for TensorFlow and Hadoop streaming), but many analysts come out of academia with extensive experience in R. Those from banking environments are typically familiar with SAS, which itself has an extensive ecosystem, including the powerful (and relatively expensive) SAS Enterprise Miner.

Some companies allow analysts to choose their own language for prototyping models, but require that any model deployed to a production environment first be coded in a compiled language such as C++ or Java and be subjected to the same rigorous testing and documentation requirements as all other production code. Some deploy the analytic models as **REST services**, so that the code runs separately from other production code.

Analytic tools

You can create your models from the ground up, but it is often faster (and less error prone) to use third-party analytic software, whether this be application components such as SAS's Enterprise Miner or IBM's SPSS, standalone tools such as RapidMiner or KNIME, cloud-based services such as Azure/Amazon/Google ML engine, or open-sourced libraries such as Python's scikit-learn, Spark's MLlib, Hadoop's Mahout, Flink's Gelly (for graph algorithms), etc. You'll get pre-built algorithms, which typically work well alongside custom-built R or Python code.

Choose a good visualization tool for creating charts. Excel will get you started, and languages such as R and Python have standard plotting libraries, but you'll want to progress to tools with more functionality. Specialized BI systems such as Tableau, Microsoft Power BI, Qlik (plus a few dozen others) will integrate easily with your data sources, and technical tools such as D3.js will allow you to create even more impressive and responsive charts within web browsers. Most companies use the plotting functionality of an off-the-shelf BI tool, which also provides the data integration, concurrency, governance and self-service required within an enterprise environment. Self-service capabilities are very important in BI tools, as they empower your users to explore data on their own, so choose a tool with a low learning curve.

The market for visualization software is booming, and there are rapid changes in market leadership. Vendors are improving their presentation, self-service capabilities, accessibility of diverse data sources and the analytic capabilities that they provide as value-adds. But your visualization tools will only come into their own in the hands of specialized experts. Form your analytics teams with this skill in mind. We'll return to this topic in Chapter 10.

Agile analytics

There are two main methods for project planning: waterfall and agile. Waterfall is a traditional approach in which the project is first planned in its entirety and then built from that planning. Agile is a more innovative approach in which small, multi-functional teams deliver incremental products, which eventually grow into the full solution.

The short delivery cycles in agile reduce the risk of misaligned delivery and force teams to build with an eye to modularity and flexibility. In addition, the focus within agile on cross-functional teams helps ensure that analytic initiatives are undergirded by necessary data, infrastructure and programming support, and are continuously re-aligning with business goals and insights.

Agile project management is gaining popularity, particularly in technology companies. It is especially helpful in big data analytics projects, where challenges and benefits are less clearly understood and more difficult to anticipate, and where underlying tools and technology are changing rapidly. Agile is designed for innovation, and it pairs well with big data projects, which themselves focus on agility and innovation.

In IT and analytics, agile methodologies are most often carried out using the framework called *scrum* (think rugby), which is employed in one of its forms at least five times as often as other agile frameworks.[69] Even departments outside of IT work with scrum, and it is not uncommon to see HR or marketing teams standing around scrum planning boards.

Agile methodologies are being embraced even at the highest levels within corporations, with companies embracing the principles of 'fail fast' and 'nail it, then scale it.' In the context of their recent digital initiative, General Electric (GE) has been developing what they call a 'culture of simplification': fewer layers, fewer processes and fewer decision points. They've adapted lean principles in what they call 'Fast Works.' They have broken away from many traditional annual operating cycles. As their (former) CEO Jeff Immelt said, 'in the digital age, sitting down once a year to do anything is weird; it's just bizarre.'[70]

Keep in mind

Business feedback is key to making agile work. Work in short delivery cycles and solicit frequent feedback from your stakeholders.

It's important to emphasize this once more. Don't try to solve your full problem at once. Don't try to assemble a complete, cleaned data set before starting your analysis. Spend two weeks building a 60 per cent solution using 10 per cent of the data, then get feedback on the results. Spend the next two weeks making a few improvements and then collect more feedback.

There are several advantages to such a short-cycled approach over trying to build the solution in one shot. First, you'll demonstrate to your stakeholders after just a few days that you have indeed been working and that you are still alive. Second, if you happen to be headed down the wrong path with your analysis, either because the data doesn't mean what you thought or because the problem wasn't communicated clearly, then you can correct the misunderstanding before wasting more time. Third, it's all too likely that the business priorities will change before you've completed the full project. Your short delivery cycles will allow you to cash in on the deliverable while it is still appreciated, before you start work on a now more relevant project.

Keep your analytics agile by following the following basic principles:

- Start with a minimum viable product (MVP). Make it cheap and quick, because once you get feedback from your initial results, it will almost certainly need to change.

- Learn and change quickly. Get feedback from end users as often as you can. Gain their trust and support by listening closely to their input.

- Build modular components that are fault tolerant. Consider a microservice architecture, where components are built independently and communicate through a well-defined, lightweight process. This architecture will have some cost in speed and efficiency but will improve fault tolerance and usability.

There are many books, certifications and trainings on the topics of lean, agile and scrum, as well as at least one book written entirely about lean analytics. I touch on the topics here only briefly, to emphasize the importance of working in an agile manner to effectively derive business value from big data.

Takeaways

- Analytics can be divided into four levels of increasing complexity, but even basic analytics can be extremely valuable. Start by getting your data in order and doing some spreadsheet analysis.

- A well-designed graph can give insights you won't get from a table.

- When you have a choice of analytic models, use the simplest and most intuitive.

- AI and machine learning have promises and pitfalls. Weigh the value, the risks, the costs and the alternatives.

- Analytics projects are best carried out using agile approaches.

- Leverage existing tools and technologies as far as possible, but consider the factors discussed above before making your choices.

Ask yourself

- Which of the four types of analytics does your organization utilize effectively? For those you are not already utilizing, are you hindered by lack of skills, use-cases or priority?

- Think of times when an insight jumped out at you from a graph. What data are you regularly reviewing in tables that might benefit from a graphical representation?

- Where in your organization are you using analytic models but not yet incorporating business intuition within the modelling process? Are you satisfied with the output of those models? You may need to push to bring more business insight into those models.

- How frequently do you review deliverables from your analytics projects? Which end users are testing out the intermediate deliverables for those projects?

Chapter

9

Choosing your technologies

You'll find it's become much easier to start collecting and using big data thanks to recent developments in technology, but the range of technologies can be bewildering. Do an image search for the most recent 'Big Data Landscape' and you'll see what I mean. We should never start our big data journey by focusing on technology, but we won't get far into the journey without it.

We'll talk about your **technology stack**, which is the set of components that together make up your technology solution. For example, your production stack might be Java or C++ code running on an Ubuntu (Linux) operating system, which may in turn be running code in Docker containers on HP servers, possibly cloud-based. Most components of your stack will already be in place, courtesy of your IT department.

In assembling your technology for big data, you'll need to make decisions such as:

1. What computer hardware will you use?

2. Where will that hardware be located?

3. How will you construct the data pipeline (including choice of source systems and sensors, transfer mechanisms, data cleaning processes and destination databases or applications)?

4. What software will you use: programming languages, libraries, frameworks and third-party tooling?

5. How will you deliver the results to the internal and external end users?

Some of these decisions are more critical than others, and many will be dictated or heavily influenced by your industry sector and your organization. The second question above, hardware location, is the newer consideration in the world of IT, and I'll devote more space to it below.

Choosing your hardware

Look closely at your current and projected requirements for data volume, processing and transfer. Most software applications will specify minimum and recommended hardware specs, including details of number and power of processors, memory (RAM), storage (disk) and networking capabilities. Big data solutions will often require clusters of machines, typically 3–6 to cover basic functionality, but scaling up to tens of thousands for large applications. Neural networks are fastest when run on specialized processors, such as GPUs, rather than on standard CPUs, so don't plan to re-deploy standard processors for such applications.

Choosing where your technology is located: cloud solutions

We introduced cloud computing in Chapter 5, where we described public and private clouds, the latter being when a large company dynamically allocates centralized computing resources to internal business units. Cloud technologies include hardware and software applications such as email, databases, CRM systems, HR systems, disaster recovery systems, etc.

A study by Dell reported that 82 per cent of mid-market organizations across the globe were already using cloud resources in 2015, with 55 per cent of organizations utilizing more than one type of cloud.[1] Organizations actively using cloud reported higher revenue growth rates than those who weren't. The main perceived benefits of cloud computing are outlined in Figure 9.1.

Cloud computing enables you to quickly provision cloud-based hardware, a service known as **Infrastructure as a Service** (IaaS). This is key to your big data initiatives. The underlying principle in choosing technology for big data is moving quickly and with flexibility. IaaS provides this, allowing you to scale storage and processor capacity within minutes.

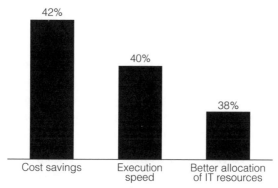

Figure 9.1 Top perceived benefits of cloud computing.[1]

Case study
984 leftover computers

To illustrate the advantage of rapidly scaling infrastructure without committing to purchase, consider Google's earlier image detection efforts. Initially built using CPUs running on 1000 computers, Google's cost for the hardware was roughly one million dollars. They subsequently redeployed the project on GPUs, which worked so much better that they were able to run the model at a fraction of the cost on just sixteen computers (roughly $20,000).[71] Most companies could not afford to make such a large hardware purchase for an experimental project, nor to explain to their finance department the hundreds of computers purchased but no longer needed.

You'll still need to install software on the cloud-based hardware (the operating system, middleware, storage, etc.), but if you want to move straight to running applications, you can utilize a **Platform as a Service (PaaS)** offering, which may be proprietary or may be an open-sourced product implemented and maintained by a service provider. In this way, your analytics programme can outsource both the hardware and the foundational software and work directly on your application.

You may have concerns regarding security in the cloud. For public clouds and **Software as a Service (SaaS)**, security is in fact the biggest barrier for companies considering the cloud. In the Dell study cited above, 42 per cent of companies not yet using cloud said security was the reason, far higher than any other reason. European companies often want to keep their data within Europe, particularly following Edward Snowden's revelations and the resulting turmoil in Europe's **Safe Harbor Provisions**.

In industries such as finance, where security, reliability and compliance are particularly critical, companies have traditionally opted to manage their own data centres to keep tighter control of security and reliability. However, earlier security concerns in these sectors continue to be alleviated by cloud providers, and companies in the financial, pharmaceutical, and oil and gas sectors have started utilizing cloud technologies.[72]

Some companies attest that running applications in the cloud leads to more secure applications, as it forces them to leave behind insecure legacy software. Being more state of the art, applications built for the cloud are generally designed with high levels of control, with better monitoring capabilities and better overall security. The cloud providers give a degree of consistency that enhances security, and they are themselves very conscious of securing their assets.

Moving, cleaning and storing your data: data pipelines

You'll need to architect your data pipeline, selecting data warehousing and middleware, such as messaging systems for transferring information in real time (e.g. Kafka, RabbitMQ, etc.)

Moving and cleaning data is generally the most time-consuming part of an analytics effort. You can purchase an **ETL** tool to do much of the heavy lifting in data processing. It should provide useful ancillary functionality, such as for documentation. A good ETL tool can make it easy to add a new data source, pulling data not only from a traditional database but also from newer sources such as web analytics servers, social media, cloud-based noSQL databases, etc.

You'll also need to select and prepare the destination database(s). As we discussed earlier, there are hundreds of database solutions to choose from. If you're deeply rooted in a vendor technology, you may want to continue within that vendor's product ecosystem, or you may consider adding new technologies, running several systems in parallel or as separate projects. Migrating from a proprietary to an open-source database can bring significant cost savings. One company recently reported cutting its cost per terabyte in half. You'll also need to invest significant effort in setting up the logical and physical structures of the database tables in a way that best fits your intended use.

Choosing software

We should emphasize again that extensive libraries for analytics have been developed for the major programming languages, and you should start your analytics effort by working with what is already available. Popular languages and tools such as Python, R, SAS and SPSS already include extensive analytic libraries with large support communities. In Python, a developer can build a neural network with only a few lines of code by leveraging existing software packages such as Keras and TensorFlow.

Don't expect to find off-the-shelf software that completely solves your analytic challenge, but existing software should give you a good head start, particularly if it integrates seamlessly with your data pipeline and automates data processing. Keep in mind that solutions still need to be customized to your problem, and you'll want to apply subject-matter expertise to engineer the model features that work best for your application. In addition, it is often the case that off-the-shelf solutions are simply implementing a common analytic model.

When purchasing analytic software, you should always ask yourself the standard questions that you would ask for any software purchase (cost, reliability, required training, etc.).

Keep in mind

Don't expect to find an off-the-shelf solution that solves your problem without substantial additional effort.

Delivery to end users

If you're building an analytic tool that will be used in a production environment, such as delivering a real-time recommendation for a customer or setting an optimal price based on real-time supply and demand, you'll need to choose a delivery technology that fits the technical requirements and constraints of your delivery end-point. For example, your web page may access content by calling a REST service on your analytic server or by executing a direct database call within the network.

Internal users will access your outputs either directly from a database, on reports or dashboards, or using a self-service BI tool. Reports and dashboards have the advantage of standardization and quality control and can be generated manually or with special-purpose software.

But data in reports ages quickly and may exclude important details. Their readers also cannot dig deeper to get more insights. This is one reason self-service BI is so important, and BI tools have come a long way over the past few years in providing this functionality. Like MS Excel but much more powerful, these self-service tools allow users to create graphs and pivot tables and explore relationships and segments not shown in other reports. Look for these self-service capabilities when choosing your BI technology.

Considerations in choosing technologies

As you select technologies for your big data projects, consider the points outlined below.

1. **Capabilities matching business requirements** Look critically at your need-to-haves vs nice-to-haves, and consider how those may develop over time. Products may be 'best in class' because of features not important for your application. Interview your stakeholders to understand requirements such as:

   - How frequently should data be refreshed?
   - What needs to happen in real time rather than batch (once daily, typically overnight)?
   - Which data sources will be accessed?

- Is it important that the system is available 100 per cent of the time?

- What technologies can your colleagues easily work with, based on their skill sets?

As you speak with technology vendors and users in other organizations, you'll become aware of additional features and use cases that may not have surfaced during your internal discussions.

You should consult a wide range of stakeholders, including:

- Budget holders, who will oversee costs and have preferences for CapEx or OpEx.

- Legal and privacy officers, who will have requirements related to data location, governance, fair use and accessibility.

- IT teams, who will help you leverage technologies and skills already in your organization (Python, for example, is commonly used across IT teams). They will also have technical requirements that you must satisfy.

- Business units, who will have requirements related to usability and delivery. Their input will certainly impact your choice of BI tools and could potentially impact any part of the big data technology stack, with requirements related to latency, accuracy, speed, concurrency, consistency, transparency or delivery.

You may need to set aside your agile mindset when choosing technology. Some solutions, after an initial test period and a limited proof of concept, require a significant deployment decision. In such cases, conduct a thorough requirements analysis before making significant investments or deployment efforts.

To illustrate, assume you work in the financial services, where security, reliability and compliance are critical. Companies in this industry have traditionally opted to manage their own data centres and keep complete control over security and reliability. They avoid early adoption of technologies, particularly open-source. Early versions of Spark and Kafka were not even an option, as they did not support SSL security protocols.

In financial services, you would have stringent requirements related to auditing, which is typically more difficult with open-source software. Whereas most companies plan their systems assuming a certain degree of system failure, you would require extreme reliability from each system component.

If you were in financial services, your big data technology choices would thus be guided by the following principles:

- You would not be an early adopter of new technologies.

- You would choose the most reliable software, regardless of whether it is open-source.

- You would maximize reliability by purchasing support.

- You would be very cautious when deciding to use cloud-based servers.

2. **Technology recommendations** You'll find it's often quite difficult to evaluate a technology. You'll see product features listed on marketing material, but you need insights into usability, performance, reliability, and the spectrum of undocumented features that will determine the success or failure of the technology within your organization.

Start by gathering insights and experiences from within your own organization and professional network. If your organization holds a Gartner or Forrester subscription, you'll want to set up analyst interviews and request relevant analyst papers. If you don't have such a subscription, you can often speak with one of these analysts at a conference. Bear in mind that their expertise may be stronger in vendor rather than open-source technologies.

Some independent thought leaders publish reviews and recommendations, but be aware they are often paid for their endorsements. Look also on the online forums, including slack channels, which provide a continuous stream of insights into technologies. These are frequented by some very knowledgeable practitioners, and user voting systems help keep quality high. In fact, the developers of the technologies are themselves often active on such forums.

Take care when attempting to replicate solutions chosen by others. Small differences in requirements can lead to completely different technology requirements. To illustrate, Spark is a widely referenced technology for streaming analytics, so we may see frequent mention of it online. But because Spark processes data in micro batches, it is generally not appropriate for solutions requiring a latency of under 500 milliseconds ($\frac{1}{2}$ second), and Apache Flink, a technology that originated in Germany, would probably be more appropriate for such applications.

3. **Integration with existing technology** Consider how you'll integrate your analytic solution internally as well as with your customers' technologies. Try to choose solutions that are modular (and hence provide more versatility). However, the pricing and usability benefits of packaged capabilities, combined with automated data transfer features, may make more coupled solutions attractive. Larger vendors tend to create solutions that span multiple applications, including basic analytics within a visualization tool (e.g. Tableau), machine learning within a cloud environment or a larger software suite (e.g. Microsoft, SAS or IBM), ETL and delivery solutions coupled with a data warehouse (Microsoft's BI stack) or AI capabilities within a CRM system (Salesforce's Einstein). For such applications, you'll want to consider whether such an offering fits your requirements in a way that better optimizes data flow or minimizes incremental software costs. Understand the technology platforms of your target B2B customers, which may lead you to develop integrations with or parallel solutions within those technologies or cloud environments.

4. **Total cost of ownership** Many organizations see cost as a large barrier to using big data. In Dell's 2015 survey, the top barriers to increasing the use of big data included the costs of IT infrastructure and the cost of outsourcing analysis or operations. Consider both direct and indirect costs, including licensing, hardware, training, installation and maintenance, system migration and third-party resources. Your IT department should already be familiar with this costing process, having performed similar analysis for existing technology.

   These costs continue to fall, and if you've done your homework in preparing your business case, you should be able to choose the projects and solutions that will result in positive ROI.

5. **Scalability** Consider how the technology can handle increases in data, replications, number of users and innovative data

sources. Consider also how the licensing model scales. The license for BI tools may be manageable when deployed to a dozen users, but prohibitive at the point where you want to empower several hundred employees with its self-service capabilities. A lack of planning in this area can lead to some painful budgeting moments later.

6. **Extent of user base** If you choose a fringe technology, it will impact your ability to find external support as well as to hire and train internal staff to operate the technology. The broader the adoption of the technology, particularly within your geography and industry sector, the more likely you will be able to hire qualified staff. There will also be more support available, both from third parties and from online forums such as stack overflow and slack groups. Similarly, a widely used, open-source technology is more likely to be kept up to date and to have bugs and usability issues quickly flagged and repaired.

7. **Open source vs proprietary** If you use open-source technology, you'll be able to quickly leverage the efforts of the wider community and save development time and licensing fees. As we mentioned above, your situation may dictate that you use proprietary technologies considered to be tried and true, and which come with strong service-level agreements.

8. **Industry buzz** Recruiting talent within the big data and data science domains is very difficult. Using the newest software frameworks, databases, algorithms and libraries will increase your ability to recruit top talent.

9. **Future vision of the technology** If your organization is an early technology adopter, you'll want to give preference to technologies that are quick to integrate and adapt to the technology space around them. For example, we mentioned earlier how Python is often the first language supported by new big data technologies, but that many algorithms in academia are developed in R. In addition, early consumers of new data types will want to choose an ETL or BI tool known to quickly add new data sources.

Ask vendors about their forward-looking visions. One of Gartner's two axes in their Magic Quadrant is 'completeness of vision,' which incorporates vendors' product strategies.

10. **Freedom to customize the technology** Will you be satisfied using the technology out of the box, or will you want to view and modify the code? If you are integrating the technology into a product for resale, check the licensing restrictions.

11. **Risks involved with adopting a technology** Cutting-edge technologies will be less well tested, and hence higher risk. An outsourced *as a Service* brings additional reliance on third parties, and vendor solutions depend on vendor support.

Big data technologies are fascinating, and they are developing rapidly. But you can't build a programme on technology alone. In the next chapter, I'll talk about the most critical resource you'll need, which is also the most difficult to secure: your analytics team.

Takeaways

- You'll need to make choices related to hardware, use of cloud, data transfer, analytic tools and data delivery (BI).
- Companies are increasing use of cloud solutions, but some concerns remain.
- As-a-Service offerings can free you to focus on your core differentiators.
- Stakeholder requirements and preferences will play a crucial role in technology decisions, particularly for BI tooling.
- Consider several important factors as you decide between competing technologies.

Ask yourself

- What parts of your infrastructure and software could you replace with as-a-Service offerings to allow you to focus more on your core differentiators?
- Are you experiencing integration difficulties from utilizing too many different technologies? What steps are you taking to assess these difficulties and to standardize your technology where necessary? Consider the tradeoff between costs and benefits for such a process.

- Who in your company or professional network can provide you with broad, unbiased insights into available technologies? Consider what industry conferences might be helpful in this.

- Consider your organization's growth projections. How long will it be before the technologies you are using today are either unable to handle your data needs or become prohibitively expensive for the scale you'll need to use them at?

Chapter

10

Building your team

Building a good team is always difficult. What makes it even more difficult for big data and data science are:

- severe shortages of qualified talent;
- lack of recruiter experience scoping and recruiting these roles; and
- the difficultly of staffing innovative projects with which few or no candidates have experience.

The skill shortage for big data and data science has lasted several years. I've heard in-house recruiters complain about it, and I've seen it highlighted as a major theme at industry events. Service providers and consultants have seen the mismatch in supply and demand and many are rebranding existing staff to sell services they are, in fact, unable to deliver.

In this chapter, I'll cover key roles related to big data and data science, as well as considerations for hiring or outsourcing those roles. To start, consider the mystically titled role of 'data scientist'.

Data scientists

This relatively new job title has enveloped a dozen traditional job titles and taken on a life of its own. Whereas accountants may be 'chartered', physicians may be 'licensed' and even first-aid workers are 'certified', anyone can call themselves a 'data scientist'.

The term 'scientist' has traditionally referred to creative individuals who apply any available tool to observe and interpret the world around them. The term 'engineer' would then be someone trained in a specific application. With the changes in available data sources and methodologies, such as the application of AI to unstructured big data stores, we found ourselves needing to move beyond our pre-defined (engineering) analytic methods, such as statistics and numerical optimization, and creatively apply a wide range of tools to a wide range of data sources: tools such as neural networks, support vector machines, hidden Markov models, calculus-based optimization, linear and integer programming, network flow optimization, statistics, and additional methods that have proven useful within the broad fields of data mining and artificial intelligence. We apply these methods to any data we can find, not only the familiar data within corporate files but also web logs, email records, machine sensor data, video images and social media data. Thus, the term 'science' became more appropriate for a field where practitioners were creatively moving beyond traditional methodologies.

Today we use the term 'data scientist' to encompass not only those experts who are creatively expanding the use of data but also anyone who ten years ago might have been called a statistician, a marketing analyst or a financial analyst. We have created a term so rich in meaning that it has become almost meaningless.

The *Harvard Business Review* wrote in 2012 that data scientists had 'the sexiest job of the twenty-first century'.[73] Glassdoor, a career portal, listed data scientist as the best job in America for both 2016 and 2017.[74] It is thus not surprising that recent years have seen a flood of semi-qualified job candidates entering the field, further muddying the recruitment waters. Data from the job portal Indeed.com shows a levelling out of data science positions over the past few years (Figure 10.1), while the number of job candidates for such positions grew steadily (Figure 10.2), which is not to say that the number of qualified candidates has increased. This surge in job seekers emphasizes the importance of properly screening candidates.

Despite its inherent vagueness, you'll want to include the term 'data scientist' in your analytic role descriptions for purposes of keyword search, followed by concrete details of what you really

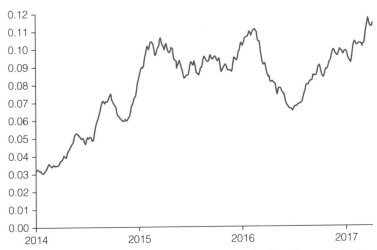

Figure 10.1 Percentage of job postings including the term 'Data Scientist.'

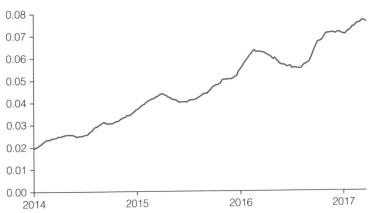

Figure 10.2 Percentage of candidates searching for 'Data Scientist' positions.[75]

need in the candidate. You may see this job title connected to any of the specific roles I'll describe in the next section. Internally, focus your recruitment efforts on the specific competencies you need, rather than on the term 'data scientist'.

Let's look now at the specific job roles you'll want to fill for your big data and data science initiatives.

Data and anaytics roles you should fill

Platform engineers

If you're not utilizing Infrastructure as a Service or Platform as a Service offerings, you'll need staff to get your specialized computer systems up and running, particularly the distributed computing clusters. Some common position titles related to these functions are 'systems engineers', 'site ops', and 'dev ops'.

Data engineers

Preparing data for analysis is more time consuming than doing the analysis. You'll need to Extract the data from source, Transform/clean the data, and Load it in tables optimized for retrieval and analysis (the ETL process). Specialized software will help, but you'll still waste a lot of time and see huge performance losses if you don't have specially trained people for this task.

Your data engineers should:

- Have expertise in using multi-purpose ETL tools as well as data manipulation tools for the big data ecosystem (tools with names such as Pig, Storm, etc.).

- Have expertise in designing data warehouse tables. Depending on your tooling, this may include OLAP cubes, data marts, etc. If the database tables are poorly designed, your reports and data queries may become unusable due to instability and lag. These specialists in database design will also be able to help colleagues write optimized data queries, saving development effort and reducing query execution time.

The role of data engineer has become very difficult to fill in some geographies, but if you don't get specialist data engineers, others in your team will waste time covering this critical but specialized task, with at best mediocre results. I've seen it before, and it's not pretty.

Algorithm specialists

Your most innovative projects will be done by experts using mathematics, statistics and artificial intelligence to work magic with your data. They are writing the programs that beat the world champion at Go, or recommend your next favourite movie on Netflix, or understand that now is the right time to offer the customer a 10 per cent discount on a kitchen toaster. They are forecasting your Q2 revenue and predicting the number of customers you'll see next weekend.

The people you hire for these tasks should have a strong background in mathematics, usually a degree in maths, statistics, computer science, engineering or physics, and they should have experience writing and coding algorithms in a language such as Java, Scala, R, Python or C/C++. They should preferably be experienced in object-oriented programming. If you are developing a highly specialized algorithm, such as for image or speech recognition, you will probably want someone who has completed a PhD in that area.

There are a few key skills I look for in building the team of algorithm specialists. These skills may not all be present in one person, but they should be covered within your team.

- **Expertise in statistics.** You'll use statistics in A/B testing and in forecasting and there are statistical models and techniques you'll want to consider for many other applications. Most team members will have a basic knowledge of statistics, but it's good to have someone with specialized knowledge.

- **Expertise in mathematical optimization.** You'll want to cover the bases of multivariate calculus-based methods (e.g. quasi-Newton and gradient descent), linear and integer programming, and network flow algorithms. These are important tools for certain applications, and without them you'll eventually end up pounding in screws with a hammer.

- **Expertise with a general algorithm prototyping tool.** You'll want someone who is trained on a tool such as KNIME, Rapid-Miner, H20.ai, SAS EnterpriseMiner, Azure ML, etc. and who can leverage the modelling and data processing libraries to rapidly experiment with a variety of diverse models, possibly throwing together a few ensembles (collections of models that together 'vote' on a result). For a certain classification problem, for example, they might compare results from a statistical regression vs results from a support vector machine vs results from a decision tree, quickly determining the most promising model for future development and eventual deployment.

- **Strong algorithmic coding skills.** The code you eventually put in production should be well-designed and efficient. An algorithm can run very slowly or very quickly depending on how it is coded. For this reason, you want some team members who are especially proficient at coding production-ready algorithms in your production language. Someone on the team should also have a good understanding of computational complexity, which relates to the scalability of algorithms. If doubling the problem size makes your technique 100 times slower, then your technique will not remain usable as the problem size grows.

For the algorithm specialist role, look closely at the candidates' degrees and Alma Maters. Some universities are much stronger than others. Be aware that countries differ in the effort required to earn a degree. To further complicate the matter, some universities may not be top-ranked overall but are world leaders in specific fields. You may be surprised to see the computer science programme at the University of Washington ranked above the programmes at Princeton and Harvard. Finally, keep in mind that the difference between two PhD graduates from the same school can still be wide enough to drive a truck through.

Keep in mind

Educational background and experience with well-known companies can be strong signals of candidate strength, but they should not dictate your hiring decisions.

For some roles related to algorithm development, particularly those requiring extreme innovation, we value high intelligence and creativity more than relevant experience. Several years ago, a friend interviewed at one of the world's top hedge funds. The entire interview process consisted of five to six hours of solving brain teasers, with almost no questions related to the financial markets or even coding. This company was looking for raw creative intelligence in their algorithm developers, and they trusted that the right people could learn any relevant subject matter as needed. Although this may be a viable tactic when hiring algorithm developers, it's not appropriate for roles such as data engineers and business analysts.

Business analysts

Most of the 'data scientists' that you hire will probably be what I would call 'business analysts'. These analysts are business thought partners and answer basic but important data questions asked by your business units. They typically use basic technologies to gather data and then spreadsheets to analyse the data and deliver results. In other words, these guys are great with Microsoft Excel.

There are various schools of thought as to where these analysts should be positioned within the organization, with some companies grouping them in a centralized team and some embedding them within business units.

Centrally located analysts can more easily share knowledge and can be allocated on demand to the highest priority projects. Dispersed analysts can leverage the insights and quick feedback available as part of a business team. The decentralized model probably occurs more often in small to mid-sized enterprises, as it does not require executive sponsorship but is funded at department level and justified by an expressed business need for data insights.

In either case, encourage the business analysts to keep strong lines of communication among themselves, with the algorithm developers and especially with the data engineers. The business analysts will provide valuable business insights to the algorithm developers, who in turn can propose innovative solutions to front-line challenges. The data engineers should actively assist the business analysts with data extraction, or else the analysts will waste time writing sub-optimal queries.

Web analyst(s)

Customer online behaviour is a very important data source. You can choose from a broad selection of mature web analytics products, but whichever tool(s) you choose should be managed by a trained specialist who keeps current on developments in web analytics and related technologies (including browser and mobile OS updates).

Your web analyst will oversee web and app tagging and make sure that online customer activity is collected effectively. Some web analytics tools can also collect data from any connected digital device, not only browsers and apps, and the web analyst can assist with this data consolidation. The web analyst will create conversion funnels and implement custom tagging, and will monitor and address any implementation problems that may arise, such as data errors related to browser updates. They will assist merging internal data with web analytics data, which may be done within the organization's databases or on the web analytics server.

Your web analyst will also be an expert in extracting data, creating segments, and constructing reports using available APIs and interfaces. For this reason, this person may be actively involved with A/B testing, data warehousing, marketing analysis, customer segmentation, etc.

Reporting specialists

You'll benefit greatly if you hire or train staff skilled at creating top-notch graphs and tables. This requires a mixture of art and science and should be done by people who excel in, for example:

- Selecting the table or graph most suited to the use-case. For example, trends will jump out from graphs much more quickly than from tables, but tables are better for sequential review.
- Selecting the layout and format most appropriate to the data. For example, reports with time series data shown vertically are not intuitive.
- Reducing visual clutter, freeing the recipient to focus on the most important data. This is rarely done well.
- Leveraging principles of gestalt and pre-attentive processing.
- Selecting shapes and colours that minimize confusion.

Stephen Few has written multiple books covering best practices for data visualization.[60,76–79]

On a technical level, the reporting specialists should be comfortable writing database queries to extract data from source systems, and they should be trained on your BI tool(s).

Leadership

Leadership is key to the success of your analytics programme. In the CapGemini survey referenced previously, close to half the organizations were already engaged in organizational restructuring to exploit data opportunities, and a third were appointing senior big data roles, recognizing that data opportunities spanned the breadth of their businesses.

My clients sometimes ask me to help scope requirements for and recruit analytics leadership. This 'lead data scientist' role is typically opened by the company for one of two reasons:

1. The company is looking to launch a new department to leverage data science and/or big data, or
2. The company has tried to launch such a department using existing management and has realized (the hard way) their need for fresh, specialized leadership.

I've conducted several hundred interviews for analytics roles over the nearly 20 years that I've worked in financial and business analytics, and I've screened even more CVs. The candidates with whom I've spoken have come from across the world, many having completed world-class technical graduate programmes or MBA programmes at schools such as Wharton, Chicago Booth or Oxford. It's been a real privilege to find and hire many excellent people over the years.

Filling a lead analytics role, however, is particularly challenging because of the complex requirements the candidate must satisfy.

Possession of three unrelated skill sets

The lead role requires a strong blend of technical, business and communication skills; skills that often correlate negatively. Individuals excelling technically often have proportionately less interest in mastering communication with non-technical business colleagues and may prioritize technical innovation above business value.

Breadth and depth of technical skills

From an analytics perspective, the leadership role requires both familiarity with a broad range of tools and techniques and an experience-based understanding of what is involved with in-depth technical implementations. There is certainly space in an organization for specialists in areas such as statistics, deep learning, NLP, or integer programming, but for the lead role, the right candidate must have an overview of the entire analytic tool chest, allowing them to select techniques that best address business problems and to recruit specialized talent as needed.

The leader must also be familiar with relevant tooling, including database technologies, programming frameworks, development languages and prototyping tools, examples of which were given above. The technology space is already quite broad, and it continues to expand. Properly leveraging existing technologies can easily save months or years of in-house development.

Ability to deliver results

Initiatives will almost certainly fail if the analytics leader cannot:

- understand tangible business drivers and KPIs;
- identify appropriate data science techniques, tools, and applications, typically drawn from cross-industry studies;
- execute the analytics projects in a lean manner; and
- communicate vision so as to win buy-in from peers.

The hiring process for the lead role

There are three phases through which I typically progress alongside a company recruiting the lead role.

1. **Aligning with the recruitment team** The internal recruiters are usually a pleasure to work with and are typically eager to learn about new profiles. The lead analytics role is almost always new to them in its skill sets, technologies, background and business experience, and so we work closely over multiple sessions to scope the role, identify appropriate distribution channels, and review candidates.

    It's important to think about salary early in the process, as you may not realize the high premium this role commands in the job market. You'll lose qualified candidates if it takes too long to bring salary expectations to market levels.

2. **Finding strong candidates** This is perhaps the most challenging part. You are looking for someone to take complete ownership of your analytics programme, and, depending on your organizational structure, possibly of data governance. Create a set of general and detailed questions spanning the competencies you feel are most important for the position and give the candidate space in the interview to communicate their own passions, ambitions and experience.

You'll find it difficult or impossible to probe the candidates' analytics expertise yourself, but you can focus on past achievements and the candidate's vision for this position. Bring in your technology team to assess the candidate's understanding of technology, and your business leaders to make sure they are comfortable with communication and business acumen.

3. **Landing the candidate** The top candidates will have many job options. Offer a competitive salary and follow up closely with the candidate to quickly address any ancillary concerns.

For lead data science roles, my experience is that strong candidates will be drawn most by the opportunity to work with interesting and abundant data and by the opportunity to contribute in creative and meaningful ways without heavy-handed interference.

Recruiting the data team

Because big data roles have only existed for a few years, many external recruitment firms struggle to understand the profiles they are being asked to fill. Some third-party recruiters I've spoken with are not able to distinguish between a data engineer and an algorithm developer. They are not familiar enough with the rapidly changing technology landscape to match skills and experience on a C.V. with requirements for a posting, let alone to assist you in writing specifications that best describe your needs. They may struggle to present the role in a way that is attractive to top talent and may end up recycling old job postings, demonstrating to candidates a disconnect with modern technology.

Generalist recruitment firms compete with internal recruiters at technology companies, who are actively poaching specialist recruiters. You should rethink your traditional methods of sourcing candidates, broaden your network of third-party recruiters and make conscious efforts to help internal recruiters understand the nature of the new roles as well as the preferences and quirks of target candidates. Send your recruiters to a good data conference to get them up to speed with concepts and terminology and to help them in networking.

Case study
Analytics staffing at 'the most promising company in America'

Instacart, an online company providing same-day grocery deliveries, was founded in Silicon Valley in 2012 by a former Amazon employee. In 2015, Forbes called it 'the most promising company in America'. By 2017, it had grown to over 1000 employees and a market valuation of several billion dollars.

Instacart uses machine learning for several important applications, such as to decrease order fulfilment time, plan delivery routes, help customers discover relevant new products, and balance supply with demand.

In a recent interview, Jeremy Stanley, Vice President of Data Science, elaborated on analytics staffing within Instacart. Their data people are divided into two categories:

1. Business analysts, who use analytic methods to help guide strategy and business decisions.

2. Machine learning engineers, who are embedded within functional teams to build software that will be deployed into production.

They only hire ML engineers with solid experience, but they have also trained internal software engineers to be ML engineers, a process that typically takes about one year. Although none of their business analysts have transitioned to the role of ML engineer, they estimate it would take two to three years of training to teach these business analysts the development skills necessary to write production-ready ML software.

They feel recruitment is most difficult at the top of the funnel (finding the candidates), but is helped by:

1. Tapping the networks of current employees.
2. Publicly talking about interesting projects (they recently wrote a blog post about a deep learning application).
3. Giving back to the community by open-sourcing projects and data sets and by hosting competitions.

Their decentralized model pushes much of the hiring and mentoring to the data science VP, who estimates his time is evenly split between hiring, mentoring and hands-on project work.

Hiring at scale and acquiring startups

The hiring challenge is compounded when it needs to happen at scale. You may want to staff up rapidly after you've established the value of an analytics effort through a proof of concept. According to a recent McKinsey survey of 700 companies, 15 per cent of operating-profit increases from analytics were linked to hiring experts at scale.[80]

You can fill some positions by re-allocating internal resources, particularly those positions that require only general software development skills or a general analytics background. For more specialized skill sets, particularly within AI, companies often fill staffing needs by acquiring smaller, specialized companies, particularly startups. We saw this at eBay in 2010, when eBay quickly scaled its pool of mobile developers by purchasing Critical Path Software. We see it still within AI, with Google's acquisition of DeepMind (75 employees at the time) and Uber's acquisition of Geometric Intelligence (15 employees). Salesforce, which is pushing its AI offering in its Einstein product, acquired key AI staff in 2016 through its acquisition of the Palo Alto-based AI startup MetaMind, with the expressed goal to 'further automate and personalize customer support, marketing automation, and many other business processes' and to 'extend Salesforce's data science capabilities by embedding deep learning within the Salesforce platform.'[81]

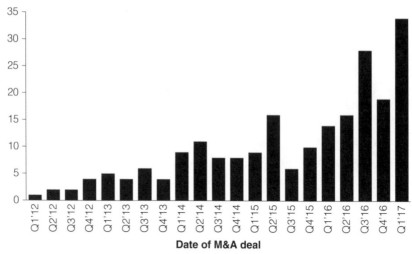

Figure 10.3 Rate at which AI companies have been acquired 2012–2017.[84]

GE, a company with over 10,000 software developers and archi-
tects, recently launched an IoT software platform called *Predix*.
They grew the Predix team from 100 employees in 2013 to 1000
employees in 2015, with plans to retrain their entire global software team on the new platform.[82] This rapid growth was also
fuelled by acquisition. They hired the co-founder of key technology provider Nurego as Predix general manager, subsequently
acquiring the entire company.[83]

Figure 10.3 illustrates the increasing rate at which AI companies
have been acquired over the last few years.

Outsourcing

You can bring external resources to supplement your in-house
staff or you can outsource entire projects or services.

Outsourcing projects facilitates agile development and allows you
to focus on your core strengths. In terms of agility, outsourcing
allows you to quickly secure very specific expertise in technologies and data science applications. A third party may be able to
start work on a project within a few days or weeks, rather than the
several months sometimes needed for internal resources that
would need to be re-allocated or recruited (both of which are difficult for proofs-of-concept).

Owing to their specialized experience, a small team of externals might complete a proof of concept within a few weeks, whereas an internal team without comparable experience could easily take several months and would be more likely to fail. This tremendous boost in speed allows you to quickly determine which analytic initiatives bring value and to start benefiting as soon as possible.

The daily cost of external resources may be several times higher than internal salaries, but when you consider the difference in development time, they may well be more cost-effective. When you move the technology from proof of concept to production, you will want to move the expertise in-house but will then have the business case to support the long-term investment.

Many organizations hire externals to supplement in-house staff, putting externals within their internal teams. Supplementing staff with externals serves three purposes.

1. It provides quick access to otherwise difficult-to-hire talent.

2. It gives you the flexibility to cut headcount when necessary (this is particularly valuable in countries with strong labour laws, such as within Europe).

3. It impacts your financials, lowering headcount and providing options to move OpEx to CapEx, both of which may be interesting for investors.

Keep in mind

Bringing in external experts may be the best way to jump-start a project or do a proof of concept.

A word of caution on outsourcing: it can be quite difficult to find high-quality data science consultants. Quality varies significantly even within the same company. Since your projects will by nature be R&D efforts, there is always a chance they will result in little or no tangible benefit, regardless of the strength of the analyst. Thus, it is especially important to maximize your odds of success by bringing in the right people. If possible, look for boutique consulting firms, where the company owners are involved in monitoring each project.

In the end, if you've managed to assemble a strong internal team and a reliable set of externals to call on when needed, you've probably done better than most of your peers.

For small companies

If you are leading a smaller company or working alone, you probably won't have the resources or the requirements for a full data team. With only a few end users, you won't be as reliant on the skills of specialized data engineers. You also won't have enough consumers of reports and dashboards to justify hiring a reporting specialist, and you'll probably not have the resources to commit to a full machine learning project.

Your 'minimum viable product' for a data team in a small company would be to place the web analytics responsibility within your marketing team and to hire an analyst who can cover business analytics and reporting. The minimum skills for this analyst are:

- A strong mathematical background, including an understanding of basic statistics.
- Database skills, including experience working in SQL (standard query language).
- Good communication skills, including the ability to create clear graphs and tables.
- The ability to be a thought partner in solving business problems.

Although you typically won't launch internal machine learning projects, at this stage you can still take advantage of the pay-per-use offerings of some of the larger vendors without needing to understand how they work. Examples include the image and text recognition software of Google Cloud Vision API, Salesforce Einstein and Amazon AI.

Takeaways

- The term 'data scientist' is too broad to be useful in recruiting.
- There are 6–7 key skills you should have in your team for big data and data science projects.
- Recruiting analytics leadership is difficult, but important.
- Traditional recruiters may lack the expertise to recruit the roles you need.

- Consultants can be extremely helpful in starting new initiatives, but carefully check whether they have the relevant skills.
- Larger companies are increasingly scaling their analytics talent through acquisitions.

Ask yourself

- Which of your recruiters (in-house or external) understand the requirements for each of the seven data roles described in this chapter? If none, start speaking with new agencies.
- Who is the most senior person in your organization with a vision for data and analytics? Many companies are appointing C-level leadership in data and analytics. How would such a role fit within your organization?
- If you were to acquire a smaller, specialized company to quickly build your analytics capacities, what would that company look like? Think of location, size and skill set.

Chapter

11

Governance and legal compliance

You have three primary concerns for securing and governing your data:

1. Proper collection and safeguarding of personal data.
2. Internal governance of your own data.
3. Complying with local laws and law enforcement in each jurisdiction in which you operate.

This last one can be a huge headache for multinationals, particularly in Europe, where the General Data Protection Regulation, effective May 2018, carries with it fines for violations of up to 4 per cent of global turnover or 20 million euros (whichever is larger). The EU will hold accountable even companies headquartered outside of Europe if they collect or process data of sufficient numbers of EU residents.

Regardless of legal risk, you risk reputational damage if society perceives you as handling personal data inappropriately.

Personal data

When we talk about personal data, we often use the term **personally identifiable information (PII),** which, in broad terms, is data that is unique to an individual. A passport or driver's license number is PII, but a person's age, ethnicity or medical condition is not. There is no clear definition of PII. The IP address of the browser used to visit a website is considered PII in some but not all legal jurisdictions.

There is increased awareness that identities can be determined from non-PII data using data science techniques, and hence we speak of 'quasi-identifiers', which are not PII but can be made to function like PII. You'll need to safeguard these as well, as we'll see in the Netflix example below.

Identify all PII and quasi-identifiers that you process and store. Establish internal policies for monitoring and controlling access to them. Your control over this data will facilitate compliance with current and future government regulations, as well as some third-party services which will refuse to process PII.

PII becomes sensitive when it is linked to private information. For example, a database with the names and addresses of town residents is full of PII but is usually public data. A database of medical conditions (not PII) must be protected when the database can be linked to PII. Jurisdictions differ in their laws governing what personal data must be protected (health records, ethnicity, religion, etc.). These laws are often rooted in historic events within each region.

There are two focus areas for proper use of sensitive personal data: data privacy and data protection.

- **Data privacy** relates to what data you may collect, store and use, such as whether it is appropriate to place hidden video cameras in public areas or to use web cookies to track online browsing without user consent.

- **Data protection** relates to the safeguarding and redistribution of data you have legally collected and stored. It addresses questions such as whether you can store private data of European residents in data centres outside of Europe.

Privacy laws

If you're in a large organization, you will have an internal privacy officer who should be on a first name basis with your data and analytics leader. If you don't have a privacy officer, you should find resources that can advise you in the privacy and data protection laws of the jurisdictions in which you have customer bases or data centres.

Each country determines its own privacy and data protection laws, with Europe having some of the most stringent. The EU's

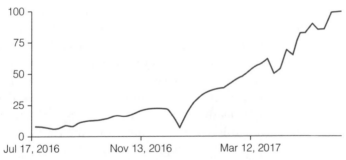

Figure 11.1 Increase in worldwide online searches for 'GDPR.'
Source: Google Trends: July 2016–June 2017.

Data Protection Directive of 1995 laid out recommendations for privacy and data protection within the EU, but, before the activation of the EU-wide General Data Protection Regulation (GDPR) in May 2018, each country was left to determine and enforce its own laws. If you have EU customers, you'll need to become familiar with the requirements of the GDPR. Figure 11.1, which shows the rapid rise in number of Google searches for the term 'GDPR' since January 2017, demonstrates that you won't be alone in this.

The extent to which privacy laws differ by country has proven challenging for multinational organizations, particularly for data-driven organizations that rely on vast stores of personal data to better understand and interact with customers. Within Europe over the past years, certain data that could be collected in one country could not be collected in a neighbouring country, and the personal data that could be collected within Europe could not be sent outside of Europe unless the recipient country provided data protection meeting European standards.

Keep in mind

Privacy and data protection laws vary by legal jurisdiction, and you may be subject to local laws even if you don't have a physical presence there.

The European Union's Safe Harbour Decision in 2000 allowed US companies complying with certain data governance standards to transfer data from the EU to the US. The ability of US companies to safeguard personal data came into question following the Edward Snowden affair, so that, on 6 October 2015, the European Court of Justice invalidated the EC's Safe Harbour Decision, noting that 'legislation permitting the public authorities to have access on a generalized basis to the content of electronic communications must be regarded as compromising the essence of the fundamental right to respect for private life.'[85] A replacement for Safe Harbou, the EU–US Privacy Shield, was approved by the European Commission nine months later (July 2016).

The United States tends to have laxer privacy laws than Europe, with some exceptions. There is an interesting example dating back to the late 1980s, when federal circuit judge Robert Bork had been nominated for the US Supreme Court. Bork, a strict constitutionalist, had previously argued that Americans only have such privacy rights as afforded them by direct legislation. This strong statement prompted a reporter to walk into a Washington D.C. video rental store and ask the manager on duty for a look at Bork's video rental history. He walked out of the store with a list of the 146 tapes the judge had checked out over the preceding two years. He subsequently published that list of tapes.[86] Amazingly, all of this was legal at the time. As it happened, the list contained nothing scandalous, but the US Congress, which had watched in awe as this saga unfolded, quickly penned and passed the Video Privacy Protection Act of 1988, making video rental history an explicitly protected class of data in the USA.

Organizations can run afoul of the law by improperly handling personal data even when it is not PII and not linkable to PII. In early 2017, US television maker Vizio paid a settlement of $2.2 million for secretly recording and selling the (anonymized) viewing history from its brand of televisions. Not only did this privacy violation cost them financially, it also made international headlines.[87]

Data science and privacy revelations

To protect yourself from legal and reputational risk, you'll need more than just an understanding of laws. You'll need to understand how customers perceive your use of data, and you'll need to be conscious of how data science techniques can lead to unintended legal violations.

When Target used statistical models to identify and target pregnant shoppers, they were not collecting private data, but they were making private revelations with a high degree of accuracy. They weren't breaking laws, but they were taking a public relations risk.

Case study
Netflix gets burned despite best intentions

Another American company got itself into trouble by not realizing how data science techniques could de-anonymize legally protected data. In 2006, video streaming company Netflix was 9 years old and had grown to roughly 6 million subscribers. It had developed a recommendation engine to increase engagement and was looking for ways to improve those recommendations. In a stroke of apparent genius, Netflix came up with the Netflix Prize: $1 million to the team that could develop a recommendation algorithm capable of beating Netflix's own by a margin of at least 10 per cent. To support the effort, Netflix released anonymized rental histories and corresponding ratings for 480,000 viewers. Remember that the Video Privacy Protection Act of 1988 forbade them to release rental histories linked to individuals, but these were anonymized.

Things moved quickly following Netflix's release of data on 2 October 2006. Within six days, a team had already beaten the performance of Netflix's own recommendation algorithm by a small margin. Within a few weeks, however, a team of researchers from the University of Texas had also hit a breakthrough. They had de-anonymized some of the anonymized rental histories. The researchers had carried out what is called a **linkage attack**, linking nameless customer viewing histories to named individuals from online forums using reviews common to both Netflix and the forums.

The saga played out for another three years, at which point a team reached the 10 per cent improvement mark and won the Netflix Prize. Shortly thereafter, a class action lawsuit was filed against Netflix, accusing it of violating privacy laws. Netflix settled out of court and understandably cancelled their scheduled follow-up competition.

It's interesting to compare these examples, as no laws were broken by Target, but the company took reputational risk through non-transparent use of personal information. Netflix, on the other hand, aligned its efforts in a very open and transparent way with the interests of customers, in this case to arrive at better video recommendations. There was little reputational risk, but there were legal consequences.

Other companies and even governments have fallen victim to such 'linkage attacks', in which linking data sources allows attackers to compromise privacy measures. If your projects require you to distribute anonymized personal information, you can apply techniques in *differential privacy*, an area of research in methods to protect against linkage attacks while maintaining data accuracy for legitimate applications. You may need this even for internal use of data, as laws are increasingly limiting companies' rights to use personal data without explicit consent.

Be aware that the behavioural data you are storing on your customers may hide more sensitive information than you realize. To illustrate, the *Proceedings of the National Academy of Sciences* documented a study conducted on the Facebook Likes of 58,000 volunteers. The researchers created a model that could, based only on a person's 'Likes', identify with high accuracy a range of sensitive personal attributes, including:

- sexual orientation;
- ethnicity;
- religious and political views;
- personality traits;
- intelligence;
- happiness;
- use of addictive substances;
- parental separation;
- age; and
- gender.

By analysing the Facebook Likes of the users, the model could distinguish between Caucasians and African Americans with a 95 per cent accuracy.[88]

So we see that two of the most fundamental tools within data science: the creative linking of data sources and the creation of insight-generating algorithms, both increase the risk of revealing sensitive personal details within apparently innocuous data. Be aware of such dangers as you work to comply with privacy laws in a world of analytic tools that are increasingly able to draw insights from and identify hidden patterns within big data.

Data governance

Establish and enforce policies within your organization for how employees access and use the data in your systems. Designated individuals in your IT department, in collaboration with your privacy officers and the owners of each data source, will grant and revoke access to restricted data tables using named or role-based authorization policies and will enforce these policies with security protocols, often keeping usage logs to verify legitimate data usage. If you are in a regulated industry, you will be subject to more stringent requirements, where data scientists working with production systems may need to navigate a half dozen layers of security to get to the source data. In this case, you'll want to choose an enterprise big data product with features developed for high standards of security and compliance.

Adding a big data repository to your IT stack may make it more difficult to control access to, usage of and eventual removal of personal information. In traditional data stores, data is kept in a structured format and each data point can be assessed for sensitivity and assigned appropriate access rights. Within big data repositories, data is often kept in unstructured format ('schema on read' rather than 'schema on write'), so it is not immediately evident what sensitive data is present.

You may need to comply with right to be forgotten or right to erasure laws, particularly within Europe, in which case you must delete certain personal data on request. With big data stores, particularly the prevalent 'data lakes' of yet-to-be-processed data, it's harder to know where personal data is stored in your systems.

GDPR will limit your use of data from European customers, requiring express consent for many business applications. This will limit the efforts of your data scientists, and you'll also be accountable under 'right to explanation' laws for algorithms that impact customers, such as calculations of insurance risk or credit score. You will likely need to introduce new access controls and audit trails for data scientists to ensure compliance with GDPR.

A full discussion of GDPR is beyond the scope of this book, and we've barely touched on the myriad other regulations in Europe and around the world. Also (quick disclaimer) I'm not a lawyer. Connect with privacy experts knowledgeable in the laws of the jurisdictions in which you operate.

Keep in mind

Laws restrict how you can use personal data, even if you have a right to collect and store that data.

Governance for reporting

Moving on from the topics of legal compliance and data protection, I'll briefly touch on an optional governance framework, which should reduce internal chaos in your organization and ease the lives of you and your colleagues. You should develop and maintain a tiered governance model for how internal reports and dashboards are assembled and distributed within your organization. Most organizations suffer tremendously from not having such a model. Executives sit at quarter-end staring in dismay at a collection of departmental reports, each of which defines a key metric in a slightly different way. At other times, a quick analysis from an intern works its way up an email chain and may be used as input for a key decision in another department.

From my experience, you'll spare yourself tremendous agony if you develop a framework for:

1. Unifying definitions used in reports and dashboards.
2. Clarifying the reliability and freshness of all reports and dashboards.

One way to do this is to introduce a multi-tiered certification standard for your reports and dashboards. The first tier would be self-service analysis and reports that are run against a development environment. Reports at this level should never leave the unit in which they are created. A tier one report that demonstrates business value can be certified and promoted to tier two. Such a certification process would require a degree of documentation and consistency and possibly additional development, signed off by designated staff. Tier-two reports that take on more mission-critical or expansive roles may be promoted to a third tier, etc. By the time a report lands on the desk of an executive, the executive can be confident of its terminology, consistency and accuracy.

Takeaways

- It is important that you identify and govern your use of personally identifiable information (PII) and quasi-identifiers.
- Establish and enforce governance and auditing of internal data usage.
- Laws related to privacy and data governance differ greatly by jurisdiction and may impact your organization even if it does not have a physical presence within that jurisdiction.
- Europe's GDPR will have a strong impact on any company with customers in the EU.
- Linkage attacks and advanced analytic techniques can reveal private information despite your efforts to protect it.
- Creating a tiered system for your internal reports and dashboards can provide consistency and reliability.

Ask yourself

- What measures are you taking to protect personally identifiable information (PII) within your systems, including protection against linkage attacks? Make sure you are compliant with regional laws in this area and are not putting your reputation at risk from privacy infringement, even if legal.
- If you have customers in Europe, what additional steps will you need to take to become compliant with GDPR? Remember that GDPR fines reach 4 per cent of global revenue.

- If your organization does not have a privacy officer, whom can you consult for questions related to privacy and data protection laws? There are global firms that can provide advice spanning multiple jurisdictions.

- When was the last time you reviewed an important internal report and realized the terminology used was unclear or the data was inaccurate? What steps did you take to address the problem? Perhaps you want to initiate an internal reporting governance programme, such as the one outlined in this chapter.

Chapter

12

'This is something I got wrong. I thought it was all about technology. I thought if we hired a couple thousand technology people, if we upgraded our software, things like that, that was it. I was wrong' —*Jeff Immelt, (former) CEO of General Electric.*[70]

Launching the ship – successful deployment in the organization

Successful data initiatives can bring tremendous business and scientific value, but many die on the launch pad because of inadequate preparation, internal resistance or poor programme management. How can you raise the odds that your data initiative will succeed? What principles can help reduce the cost and effort required?

We start by presenting an unfortunate case study of an ambitious big data project, which was launched with significant media hype, but which ended in painful failure.

Case study
The 62-million-dollar failure

You probably first heard of IBM's artificial intelligence program Watson in 2011, when it beat two living, breathing humans to win the popular American gameshow *Jeopardy*. Two years later, IBM proposed a more noble use for its champion AI program, teaming up with the M.D. Anderson Cancer Center at the University of Texas in a highly publicized project that would employ Watson in the fight against cancer. The goal was to expedite clinical decision making by having Watson match patients to archives of documented clinical trials. The world watched in expectation for the coming revolution in cancer treatment.

By the end of 2016, however, the project had proven to be a failed investment: $62 million plus significant expenditure of

▶

internal resources at the Anderson Cancer Center: staff time, technology infrastructure and administrative support. It was a sobering lesson in the reality that massively promising projects can become massive failures.

Indications are that this was not a failure of big data or of Watson technology but rather of poor project execution. A University of Texas audit cited numerous problems related to service providers, and it seems Watson was never even successfully integrated with the medical centre's new electronic medical records system.

In hindsight, experts realized there was apparently *not enough data* for Watson in this application, even if it had been successfully integrated with Anderson systems. Because so many treatment options have not yet been explored in the medical literature, and because there were relatively few high-quality clinical trials on record, Watson did not have sufficient research literature to draw on. The original project motivation was that Watson could process every article ever written to produce the best recommendation for treatment, but the reality was that oncologists often need to choose between drugs that have never been directly compared in randomized trials.

Mary Chris Jaklevic, a healthcare journalist who reported on the Watson–Anderson failure in 2016, highlighted the extreme mismatch between media hype about the project's potential and the complete failure of the project to produce results. She ended with a point we should take to heart in this rapidly developing world of big data and AI: '. . . make a habit of pointing out gaps between what's claimed and what's been demonstrated to work.'[89]

Why our projects fail

Although most organizations won't make headlines with such expensive failures, relatively few are successful in making a breakthrough in their analytics programs. In a recent survey of leaders innovating in big data analytics, three quarters reported revenue or cost improvements of less than 1 per cent.[90] In another study, only 27 per cent reported success in their big data initiatives.[32]

The *Harvard Business Review* describes an MIT researcher recently addressing a group of 150 machine learning enthusiasts. He started with the question, 'How many of you have built a machine learning model?' to which roughly one third raised their hands. He then asked how many had also deployed and/or used that model to generate value and then evaluated the results. None kept their hands up. None.[91]

In my experience, and in speaking with colleagues about their experiences, many organizations have taken steps, sometimes significant steps, to find new value from data and analytics, only to reap little practical benefit. Sometimes this is because the problems are very difficult, but it more often reflects problems with staffing, project management or organizational dynamics. Still, we've seen other organizations launch analytics projects and reap substantial returns.

So how can you maximize the likelihood that your big data and data science initiatives will succeed?

Here are some principles to follow.

Become data-driven

Keep asking questions about your business

Ask basic questions, such as 'What customers or products account for the top 20 per cent of our revenue?' Ask more nuanced questions, such as 'What motivates our customers to purchase?' and 'What sequences of cross-channel actions are the strongest signals that I might soon lose a valued customer?' You can come up with hundreds of questions like these. Focus on answering the ones most critical for your business.

Challenge your basic assumptions

Especially do this if you are very familiar with your business. When colleagues propose answers to your (sometimes obvious) questions, ask for data to back up those answers. In their book, *Yes, And,*[92] Kelly Leonard and Tom Yorton describe how a bit of data shattered some basic assumptions they had held about their 50-year-old Chicago theatre. When an outsider asked them why they thought their guests were coming to the theatre, they immediately responded with the obvious answer: the guests obviously wanted to see the show playing that night. The questioner then surveyed the guests, who gave very different reasons. The guests were actually using the theatre as a novelty event: to celebrate a birthday or the achievement of a business milestone, to entertain out-of-town guests, or because they had received the tickets as gifts or purchased them at charity events. Not a single patron gave the expected answer. Not a single one was there simply because they wanted to see the show playing that night. Seasoned management had been so certain and yet completely wrong in their assumptions. ('Yes, And' (p. 174). HarperCollins. Kindle Edition)

Create and monitor KPIs

If you're not keeping score, you're just practising. Don't simply monitor the obvious KPIs, such as revenue. Track your micro- and macro-conversion rates and your churn rate. Track your lead indicators, including those from customer activity. Track stickiness, including frequency metrics. Display the KPIs your teams can influence in places where they can see them. Set goals. Celebrate the goals. This part isn't rocket science.

Get new ideas

Technology applications quickly spread within industry sectors as employees change jobs or attend industry events, but to stay ahead you'll want to look at what's happening in other sectors. If you're in banking, look at what e-commerce companies are doing. If you're in e-commerce, look at what logistics companies are doing. Go to industry conferences and talk to vendors and analysts about use cases they've seen.

Organize your data

If you follow the advice above, you should very quickly become frustrated with the current state of your data systems. Hire and engage people who can shepherd and draw insights from your data. Train staff across your organization to use your BI tools, particularly self-service tools which allow them to explore data on their own. Selectively move data from silos to a central data warehouse.

Get the right people on board

Hire people who understand how to apply data science to business. Hire data scientists and hire data-driven people across the organization, ideally from the top down. The higher the level of buy-in within the organization, the better the chance that analytics initiatives will be funded and supported and that the entire organization will catch the vision. Top level buy-in is still relatively rare, as demonstrated by a recent industry survey. When CEOs were asked whether they were leading their companies' analytics agendas, 38 per cent said yes. However, when the other C-suite executives were asked, only 9 per cent said the CEO was indeed leading that agenda.[90]

Be aware that analytics efforts often illuminate internal shortcomings, some of which directly implicate powerful colleagues. Expect internal resistance, sometimes as ambiguous criticism or stalled cooperation, often appearing after the release of incriminating analysis.

A data-driven approach affects hiring and training throughout your organization, not only in data and analytics teams. Consider the case of General Electric (GE). GE started a major digital initiative around the beginning of 2010, acquiring companies and creating thousands of roles related to data science. In a recent interview,[70] GE's CEO Jeff Immelt recounted some key learnings from this process. He described how, even beyond staffing the data science roles, GE found they needed to hire thousands of new product managers and different types of commercial people. The impact of the transformation extended to onsite support and even sales people.

Keep in mind

Transforming into a data-driven organization requires changes throughout your organization. It's not enough to simply create a data and analytics team.

I have seen companies start data science initiatives by bringing in a few newly minted 'data scientists' and setting them loose to find their own way within the organization, hoping to somehow reap tangible benefits. We wouldn't do this with an IT initiative, and we shouldn't do it with an analytics initiative. Projects should be

done in project teams consisting of well-vetted staff with comple-
mentary skills who are ultimately connected in meaningful ways
with use-cases and stakeholders. The stakeholders, in turn, should
continually feed business intuition back into the development
process. This should all go without saying in a mature organization, and yet we often don't see it happening.

I would suggest you stop using the same vendors to meet your
staffing and project needs. Talk with newer, smaller companies
you haven't yet used. Your new initiatives should start small, so let
a small company with a few competent, creative professionals
help you start it. Don't expect that large service providers can provide top-notch staff for every engagement, and don't expect that
updated job titles reflect updated capabilities. One of the problems highlighted during the audit of the Watson–Anderson ship-
wreck was non-robust vendor selection.[93]

As an analytics programme matures, it will likely grow into a
hybrid of centralized teams and decentralized analysts sitting
within business units. The centralized teams will include a BI
team and one or more teams of analytics specialists. Some of the
decentralized analysts located within business units will have
originally joined those units in non-analytic roles, over time
assuming analytic responsibilities. As you transform your organization in its use of data, keep these people in their analytic roles if
they can efficiently retrieve data, ask relevant business questions,
perform basic analysis, and communicate results clearly. If not,
cut your losses and replace them in this function with more ana-
lytically adept staff.

Find senior analytics leadership who can form a vision, a roadmap,
and a team. Although an organization may organically grow in its
ability to be data-driven by hiring or re-purposing de-centralized
analysts, it will generally be limited to spreadsheet-level analytics
until it commits to recruiting a senior analytics leader and building
out a strong analytics team. Empower that team not only with the
resources and flexibility they need to collect data and build models
but also with access to stakeholders and key decision makers.

Without such a team, typically centralized, you will be very limited in your ability to recruit top analytics talent, and the talent

you do secure will repeatedly be pulled into 'urgent' business problems and have little time for long-term strategic initiatives. In addition, effectively deploying analytic projects such as recommendation engines, natural language processing, advanced customer segmentations and deep learning models will typically require the synergy of a centralized team of experts.

Break down silos

Data silos severely limit your ability to draw maximum value from your data, but you'll need extensive stakeholder management and significant technical resources to consolidate the siloed data spread across your functional units and legal entities (particularly following acquisitions). Business units tend to be protective, if not of their data then at least of their IT resources. How to best navigate this gauntlet depends on how your organization functions, but executive-level support goes a long way.

Focus on business value

It is very important to keep your data scientists focused on providing business value. There are non-technical people in your company who have developed a deep understanding of the customer, the product and the market. Your data scientists should speak with them at the very start of an analytics project. They should go back to them on a regular basis to show data and intermediate results. The business colleagues will quickly identify flawed assumptions or inappropriate interpretations of data. In some cases, they can even provide valuable assistance in constructing your analytic models.

Measure results

We talked earlier about promoting the use of KPIs within the organization, and this applies to data science efforts. Don't start a data science project unless you know why you're doing it and what it looks like when it succeeds. Are you looking to increase conversion rates? Marketing ROI? Market share? Customer lifetime value? Measure your starting point, set a target, and estimate resulting revenue gains. By the end of the year, you may have an ROI for the analytics programme itself.

Stay agile

Remember to stay agile, starting with minimum viable products (MVP) and working with short delivery cycles. It goes against our academic training, but we need to progressively work towards incomplete solutions rather than an immediate 100 per cent solution. Start your analysis on just a sample of the data. If you start by collecting and cleaning all possible data, you're no longer working with an MVP and you'll waste weeks or months before getting far enough to see any pitfalls that might exist in your approach. Start with simple models, such as decision trees, statistical regression and naïve Bayes. Refine your models once you've found applications with demonstrable business value.

As far as possible, get specialists working on specialized problems. Find people to extract and clean data who are skilled in this, rather than asking your statisticians and AI experts to do it.

Don't let your data scientists reinvent the wheel; instead leverage as much existing tooling and software as possible. Don't spend several months re-building an AI tool that is already available on a pay-per-use basis from Amazon, Google or Salesforce unless you need a custom feature or have hit a usage threshold making it more cost-effective to develop in-house. Your in-house efforts should be spent fitting existing tooling to your business.

In conclusion

The quantity and types of data available to you today present a tremendous opportunity. Understanding how to use this resource can improve your strategy, tactics and operations in more ways than you might expect, providing valuable insights, raising KPIs, reducing costs, and ultimately enabling better customer experiences. The key technologies are in place and others have already blazed trails for you to follow, often across boundaries that traditionally shielded industries from competitors. I wish you success on your journey!

Takeaways

- Many analytics projects fail or produce little value due to poor programme management or insufficient project scoping.

- It is critical to keep short feedback loops with business stakeholders and to work towards clear KPIs.
- Siloed data and internal resistance may hinder analytics projects.
- Analytics initiatives often fail without senior analytics leadership.
- Leverage existing technology, but don't expect off-the-shelf technology to deliver a complete solution.

Ask yourself

- Who in your company is allowed to make decisions based on 'gut feel' alone? Does anyone challenge this person's decisions?
- Which of your initiatives have clear KPIs and measurable targets? Remember: if you're not keeping score, you're just practising.
- If your organization keeps duplicate copies of information within different data systems, how do you guarantee that the data is consistent? Data that is copied from a source system can quickly become stale or corrupt and cause havoc with your reporting.
- Who in your organization decides which data to leave in siloed data centres and which data to collect in a central data repository? Do you have a chief data officer, or an expert in the field of master data management?
- How are you monitoring developments in the fields of data and analytics, including new technologies that you could leverage or new methods that may already be giving a competitive edge to other companies? Perhaps you'll want to attend a leading analytics conference, such as one of the Strata Data or Gartner Data and Analytics conferences.

References

1. See https://blog.dell.com/en-us/global-technology-adoption-index-2015/ (accessed 29 September 2017).
2. McKinsey (2001, May) *Big data: The next frontier for innovation, competition, and productivity.* McKinsey Global Institute.
3. See http://www.gartner.com/newsroom/id/3598917 (accessed 29 September 2017).
4. See http://home.cern/topics/large-hadron-collider (accessed 29 September 2017).
5. See http://graphics.latimes.com/towergraphic-large-hadron-collider/ (accessed 29 September 2017).
6. See http://www.atnf.csiro.au/projects/askap/index.html (accessed 29 September 2017).
7. See http://www.atnf.csiro.au/projects/askap/science.html (accessed 29 September 2017).
8. See http://www.skatelescope.org/uploaded/8762_134_Memo_Newman.pdf (accessed 29 September 2017).
9. See http://www.mkomo.com/cost-per-gigabyte-update (accessed 29 September 2017).
10. See https://nbtventures.wordpress.com/2008/05/12/moores-law-obituaries-are-premature/ (accessed 29 September 2017).
11. White, T. (2015) *Hadoop: The Definitive Guide*, 4th edition. O'Reilly Media, Sebastopol, CA, USA.
12. See http://www-03.ibm.com/ibm/history/ibm100/us/en/icons/deepblue/ (accessed 29 September 2017).
13. See http://www.asimovinstitute.org/neural-network-zoo/ (accessed 29 September 2017).
14. See https://www.bloomberg.com/news/articles/2015-10-26/google-turning-its-lucrative-web-search-over-to-ai-machines (accessed 29 September 2017).
15. 'From big data to human level intelligence' talk given at Strata NY, September 2016): see https://www.safaribooksonline.com/library/view/strata-hadoop/9781491944660/video261030.html (accessed 29 September 2017).
16. See https://research.googleblog.com/2014/11/a-picture-is-worth-thousand-coherent.html (accessed 29 September 2017).
17. See https://arxiv.org/pdf/1312.6199.pdf (accessed 29 September 2017).

18. See https://www.wsj.com/articles/how-artificial-intelligence-will-change-everything-1488856320 (accessed 29 September 2017).
19. See https://peadarcoyle.wordpress.com/tag/recommendation-systems/ (accessed 29 September 2017).
20. See https://www.sciencedaily.com/releases/2017/02/170201093613.htm (accessed 29 September 2017).
21. See https://blogs.microsoft.com/ai/2016/10/18/historic-achievement-microsoft-researchers-reach-human-parity-conversational-speech-recognition/#sm.000098vc4j1ure4jy6g22cjyx0buc (accessed 29 September 2017).
22. See http://techpresident.com/news/24599/bill-bratton-and-ideology-data-nyc-and-future-policin (accessed 29 September 2017).
23. Humby, C., Hunt, T. and Phillips, T. (2007) *Scoring Points: How Tesco Continues to Win Customer Loyalty,* 2nd edition. Kogan Page Ltd, London, Table 5.1.
24. See https://www.economicshelp.org/blog/6288/economics/uk-grocery-market-share/ (accessed 29 September 2017).
25. See https://uk.finance.yahoo.com/quote/TSCO.L (accessed 29 September 2017).
26. See http://www.nytimes.com/2012/02/19/magazine/shopping-habits.html (accessed 29 September 2017).
27. See http://delivery.acm.org/10.1145/1080000/1072204/p52-banko.pdf?ip=79.67.200.184&id=1072204&acc=OPEN&key=4D4702B0C3E38B35%2E4D4702B0C3E38B35%2E4D4702B0C3E38B35%2E6D218144511F3437&CFID=989654340&CFTOKEN=26806559&__acm__=1506501333_25bb4cb3c2aadabe7d7bf4cf2f5b391f (accessed 29 September 2017).
28. See https://www.genome.gov/sequencingcosts/ (accessed 29 September 2017).
29. See https://www.genome.gov/pages/der/seqcost2015_4.xlsx (accessed 29 September 2017).
30. See https://www.safaribooksonline.com/library/view/strata-hadoop/9781491944660/video282747.html (accessed 29 September 2017).
31. See https://digiday.com/media/washington-post-grew-digital-subscriptions-145-percent/ (accessed 29 September 2017).
32. Capgemini (2015) Big & Fast Data: The Rise of Insight-Driven Business, Capgemini, London.
33. See http://www.comscore.com/layout/set/popup/content/download/33933/1882805/version/5/file/2016_US_Cross_Platform_Future_in_Focus.pdf (accessed 29 September 2017).
34. See https://www.dsayce.com/social-media/tweets-day/ (accessed 29 September 2017).

35. See https://baymard.com/lists/cart-abandonment-rate (accessed 29 September 2017).
36. See https://www.mckinsey.com/business-functions/mckinsey-analytics/our-insights/applying-analytics-in-financial-institutions-fight-against-fraud?cid=other-eml-alt-mip-mck-oth-1704 (accessed 29 September 2017).
37. See http://supplychaininsights.com/wp-content/uploads/2012/07/Big_Data_Report_16_JULY_2012.pdf (accessed 29 September 2017).
38. See https://blog.hubspot.com/blog/tabid/6307/bid/31042/When-Lead-Scoring-Is-a-Waste-of-Marketers-Time.aspx#sm.000098vc4j1ure4jy6g22cjyx0buc (accessed 29 September 2017).
39. See http://blogs.gartner.com/doug-laney/files/2012/01/ad949-3D-Data-Management-Controlling-Data-Volume-Velocity-and-Variety.pdf (accessed 29 September 2017).
40. See https://nsa.gov1.info/utah-data-center/ (accessed 29 September 2017).
41. See https://www.youtube.com/yt/about/press/ (accessed 29 September 2017).
42. See http://journals.plos.org/plosbiology/article?id=10.1371/journal.pbio.1002195 (accessed 29 September 2017).
43. See http://www.skatelescope.org/wp-content/uploads/2011/03/SKA-Brochure.pdf (accessed 29 September 2017).
44. See http://www.skatelescope.org/uploaded/8762_134_Memo_Newman.pdf (accessed 29 September 2017).
45. See https://research.google.com/archive/gfs-sosp2003.pdf (accessed 29 September 2017).
46. http://blog.schneider-electric.com/wp-content/uploads/2016/05/IoT-and-the-Pervasive-Nature-of-Fast-Data-and-Apache-Spark.pdf (accessed 29 September 2017).
47. See https://en.wikipedia.org/wiki/Free_and_open-source_software#cite_note-8 (accessed 29 September 2017).
48. See https://en.wikipedia.org/wiki/History_of_free_and_open-source_software (accessed 29 September 2017).
49. See https://news.netcraft.com/archives/2009/02/18/february_2009_web_server_survey.html (accessed 29 September 2017).
50. See http://web.archive.org/web/20021001071727/wp.netscape.com/newsref/pr/newsrelease558.html (accessed 29 September 2017).
51. See https://projects.apache.org/timelines.html (accessed 29 September 2017).
52. See https://www.cnet.com/news/microsoft-raps-open-source-approach/ (accessed 29 September 2017).

53. *The Economist* (2017) 'How retailers are watching shoppers' emotions', 8 June.

54. See https://genius.com/Marc-andreessen-why-software-is-eating-the-world-annotated (accessed 29 September 2017).

55. See https://hbr.org/1993/01/customer-intimacy-and-other-value-disciplines (accessed 29 September 2017).

56. See http://www.dell.com/learn/us/en/uscorp1/press-releases/2015-10-13-dell-global-technology-adoption-index (accessed 5 November 2017).

57. See https://www.safaribooksonline.com/library/view/strata-hadoop/9781491944660/video282744.html (accessed 29 September 2017).

58. See http://www.mytotalretail.com/article/introducing-the-new-retail-brain/ (accessed 29 September 2017).

59. See https://www.economist.com/news/business/21720675-firm-using-algorithm-designed-cern-laboratory-how-germanys-otto-uses (accessed 29 September 2017).

60. Few, S. (2012) *Show me the Numbers: Designing Tables and Graphs to Enlighten,* 2nd edition. Analytics Press, Burlingame, CA, USA, p. 15.

61. See http://www.sciencemag.org/news/2017/04/self-taught-artificial-intelligence-beats-doctors-predicting-heart-attacks (accessed 29 September 2017).

62. See http://arxiv.org/pdf/1602.04938v1.pdf (accessed 29 September 2017).

63. See https://www.quora.com/Will-deep-learning-make-other-machine-learning-algorithms-obsolete (accessed 29 September 2017).

64. See http://www.asimovinstitute.org/neural-network-zoo/ (accessed 29 September 2017).

65. See https://www.tastehit.com/blog/google-deepmind-alphago-how-it-works/ (accessed 29 September 2017).

66. See https://www.wired.com/2016/08/an-exclusive-look-at-how-ai-and-machine-learning-work-at-apple/ (accessed 29 September 2017).

67. See http://www.gartner.com/smarterwithgartner/nueral-networks-and-modern-bi-platforms-will-evolve-data-and-analytics/ (accessed 29 September 2017).

68. See https://db-engines.com/en/ranking_categories (accessed 29 September 2017).

69. See https://hbr.org/2016/05/embracing-agile (accessed 29 September 2017).

70. See https://www.mckinsey.com/business-functions/organization/our-insights/ges-jeff-immelt-on-digitizing-in-the-industrial-space (accessed 29 September 2017).

71. See https://www.wired.com/2013/06/andrew_ng/ (accessed 29 September 2017).

72. See https://www.youtube.com/watch?v=BJtn9qkrHU0 (accessed 29 September 2017).

73. See https://hbr.org/2012/10/data-scientist-the-sexiest-job-of-the-21st-century (accessed 29 September 2017).

74. See https://www.glassdoor.com/List/Best-Jobs-in-America-LST_KQ0,20.htm (accessed 5 November 2017)

75. See https://www.indeed.com/jobtrends (accessed 29 September 2017).

76. Few, S. (2013) *Information Dashboard Design: Displaying Data for At-a-Glance Monitoring*, 2nd edition. Analytics Press, Burlingame, CA, USA.

77. Few, S. (2009) *Now You See It: Simple Visualization Techniques for Quantitative Analysis*, 1st edition. Analytics Press, Burlingame, CA, USA.

78. Few, S. (2006) *Information Dashboard Design: The Effective Visual Communication of Data*. O'Reilly Media, Sebastopol, CA, USA.

79. Few, S. (2015) *Signal: Understanding What Matters in a World of Noise*. Analytics Press, Burlingame, CA, USA.

80. See https://www.mckinsey.com/business-functions/digital-mckinsey/our-insights/straight-talk-about-big-data (accessed 29 September 2017).

81. See https://techcrunch.com/2016/04/04/saleforce-acquires-metamind/ (accessed 29 September 2017).

82. See http://www.computerweekly.com/news/2240241843/Executive-interview-GEs-software-chief-Bill-Ruh-on-value-of-an-industrial-cloud (accessed 29 September 2017).

83. See https://www.geektime.com/2017/02/09/israeli-iot-startup-nurego-gets-swallowed-up-by-general-electric/ (accessed 29 September 2017).

84. See https://www.cbinsights.com/blog/top-acquirers-ai-startups-ma-timeline/ (accessed 29 September 2017).

85. See http://eur-lex.europa.eu/legal-content/EN/TXT/?uri=CELEX%3A62014 (accessed 29 September 2017).

86. See https://www.washingtonpost.com/news/the-switch/wp/2014/04/28/how-washingtons-last-remaining-video-rental-store-changed-the-course-of-privacy-law/?utm_term=.bf475682e60e (accessed 29 September 2017).

87. See http://www.bbc.co.uk/news/technology-38889975 (accessed 29 September 2017).

88. See http://www.pnas.org/content/110/15/5802.full (accessed 29 September 2017).

89. See http://www.healthnewsreview.org/2017/02/md-anderson-cancer-centers-ibm-watson-project-fails-journalism-related/ (accessed 29 September 2017).

90. See https://www.mckinsey.com/business-functions/digital-mckinsey/our-insights/straight-talk-about-big-data (accessed 29 September 2017).

91. See https://hbr.org/2016/12/why-youre-not-getting-value-from-your-data-science (accessed 29 September 2017).

92. Leonard, K. and Yorton, T. (2015) *Yes And: How Improvisation Reverses "No, But" Thinking and Improves Creativity and Collaboration—Lessons from The Second City.* HarperBusiness, New York, p. 174.

93. UTMDACC Special Review of Procurement Procedures Related to Oncology Expert Advisor Project Report (2016, November). The University of Texas System Audit Office.

Glossary

A/B testing (split testing): A method to test which product version works best in practice. Customers are randomly divided into groups and shown different versions of a product (such as an element on a website). At the end of the test period, the results are analysed to see which versions performed best relative to one or more metrics

Algorithm: A sequence of actions followed to arrive at a result

Analytic model: One or more mathematical formulas that together approximate a phenomenon of interest

Apache Software Foundation: A non-profit US corporation consisting of a decentralized open-source community of developers. It maintains much of the software used within the big data ecosystem

Artificial intelligence (AI): A general term for a machine that can respond intelligently to its environment

Artificial neural networks (ANN): Analytic models that learn tasks by training networks of basic nodes which are linked in sometimes complex architectures

Batch job: A computer job, such as a data transfer or a computation, that is run at regularly scheduled intervals (often daily), rather than continuously

Batch processing: A process that is executed as a series of consecutive batch jobs

Beam (Apache): An open-source programming model designed to handle data movements in both batch and streaming modes

Big data ecosystem: The technologies that have been developed to store, transfer and process big data

Black-box model: An analytic model whose internal workings cannot easily be explained or understood

Business intelligence (BI): The field of technology dealing with the transfer, storage and delivery of data specifically for reporting and analysis

CapEx: Capital Expenditure. An investment whose benefit extends over a long period of time, such as durable goods or development of software that will be used for a long time. See also *OpEx*

Cloud computing: The use of hardware or software not owned by the end user but made available on demand according to some subscription model

Clustering: An analytic technique in which the data is divided into groups (clusters) in a way that attempts to group similar elements together

Concurrency: When evaluating suitability of software, concurrency refers to the number of users that can use the software simultaneously

Cross-validation: A method to validate analytic models by repeatedly splitting the test data, training the model on part of the data, and then testing its effectiveness on the remaining data

Dark data: A term for data which is generated by normal computer networks but not typically analysed

Data lakes: Any big data storage system designed to store raw data whose end use may not be known at time of collection

Data science: The practice of applying any number of analytic techniques using any number of data sources. The term implies the creative use of non-standard approaches in bringing business value

Data warehouses: Databases structured to facilitate analysis and reporting rather than to run operations

Deep learning: Utilizing artificial neural networks with many hidden layers (typically dozens or hundreds of layers)

Elastic Search: A widely used enterprise search platform, similar in functionality to Apache Solr

Ensemble: The term for a collection of analytic models producing separate outputs, which are then merged in a democratic way to produce a single output

ETL: Extract, Transfer, Load. The steps through which data is moved from source systems to a data warehouse. Sometimes executed as ELT

Exabyte: 10^{18} bytes, or 1000 petabytes

Expert systems: An AI that imitates the decision-making ability of a human expert, typically by learning and deducing facts and rules

Fast data: Data which appears at high velocity and must be received, analysed and responded to in real time

Feature engineering: Creating data fields not in the original records, but which you expect to be of explanatory value in an analytic model. An example would be calculating a field 'time since last purchase' from a database consisting only of purchase events

Flink: An open-source processing framework for streaming data

Forrester: An American market research and advisory firm

Forrester Wave: Forrester's periodic evaluations of vendors in specific technology spaces

Gartner: An American research and advisory firm specializing in IT

Gartner Hype Cycle: A branded, graphical presentation developed by Gartner for representing the maturity and adoption of various technologies

Gartner Magic Quadrants: Analysis provided by Gartner comparing vendors for various technology offerings. Typically updated annually

General Data Protection Regulation (GDPR): A comprehensive EU regulation related to privacy, data protection and fair usage of data, effective May 2018

Gigabyte (GB): 10^9 bytes, or 1000 kilobytes

Go: An ancient Chinese board game for two players. The goal is to surround the most territory with your stones

Goodness-of-fit test: A statistical test to assess how well a model fits the test data

Graphical processing unit (GPU): An electronic circuit specially designed for computer graphics or image processing

Hadoop (Apache): The foundational open-source software framework for distributed storage and processing of data. It uses HDFS for storage and MapReduce for processing

Hadoop Distributed Files System (HDFS): The distributed, scalable file system used by Hadoop

Hive (Apache): An open-source software for data warehousing on Hadoop

Infrastructure as a Service (IaaS): Computer server space, networking and load balancers that are used on a subscription basis

Internet of Things (IoT): A term for the billions of devices in use today that have embedded sensors and processors plus network connectivity

JavaScript: A high-level programming language often used in web browsers

JSON. JavaScript Object Notation. A common, human-readable data storage format

Kafka (Apache): A highly scalable open-source message queueing platform originally developed by LinkedIn and released to open-source in 2011

211

Key performance indicator (KPI): A quantifiable measure of performance often used within organizations to set targets and measure progress

Lambda architecture: A data processing architecture designed to balance the requirements of fast data and accurate data storage

Latency: The time taken for data to move between points

Linkage attack: An attempt to de-anonymize private data by linking it to PII

Machine learning (ML): The process through which an AI program self-improves by continuously learning from training data

MapReduce: The programming model used in Hadoop for spreading data processing across a computer cluster

Massively parallel processing (MPP) databases: Databases that spread data across multiple servers or nodes, which communicate via a network but do not share memory or processors

Micro-conversions: Events progressing towards a goal but which do not have significant value in themselves

Minimum viable product (MVP): A functioning product with the minimum features to satisfy early customers and generate feedback for future development

Models: See analytic model

Model training: An iterative process of adjusting model parameters to improve model fit to available data

Monte Carlo simulations: Repeatedly entering random numbers into the distributions assumed to govern a process and then studying the outcomes

Neural networks: See *artificial neural networks*

noSQL databases: Databases that allow storage and processing of data which is not necessarily in tabular form

OpEx: Operational Expenditure. An ongoing business cost. See also *CapEx*

Personally identifiable information (PII): Information that is unique to an individual, such as passport number.

Personas: A hypothesized user group with certain attributes, goals, and/or behaviours

Petabyte (PB): 10^{15} bytes, or 1000 terabytes

Platform as a Service (PaaS): Cloud services to build and maintain the middleware that runs on the computer hardware and supports software applications

Principal component analysis: A mathematical technique that can be used to reduce the number of variables in a model

Private clouds: A technology cloud maintained by and used within a single organization

Public clouds: A technology cloud maintained by a third party and made available according to some subscription model

RAM: Random access memory. Computer memory that can be accessed without touching preceding bytes

RASCI: A framework for defining project responsibility, divided into Responsible, Authorizing, Supporting, Consulting and Informed individuals

REST (Representational State Transfer) service: A simple, well-defined computer architecture often used to deliver information between computers across the web

Return on investment (ROI): A measure of the benefit of an investment. There are several ways to calculate ROI

Safe Harbour Decision: A ruling by the European Commission in 2000 which allowed US companies complying with certain data governance standards to transfer data from the EU to the US. On 6 October 2015, the European Court of Justice invalidated the EC's Safe Harbor Decision. A replacement for Safe Harbor, the EU-US Privacy Shield, was approved by the European Commission nine months later (July 2016)

Salesforce (salesforce.com): A popular, cloud-based software for managing customer data and assisting sales efforts

Self-service analytics: When end users are given the data and tools to generate their own basic analysis, pivot tables and charts

Semi-structured data: Unstructured data to which a few structured fields are added, such as adding time and location fields to free-text data

Software as a Service (SaaS): Centrally hosted software that is used on a subscription basis

Software framework: Software providing general, extendible, low-level functionality that can be leveraged by more specialized software

Solr (Apache): An open-source, stand-alone full-text search platform often used by enterprises to manage text search

Spark (Apache): A computing framework developed at Berkeley Labs which runs distributed computations over RAM memory. It has replaced Hadoop's MapReduce in many applications

Split testing: See *A/B testing*

Standard Query Language (SQL): The standard language for inserting and retrieving data from relational databases

Technology stack: A collection of software components that interact to form a complete technology solution

Terabyte (TB): 10^{12} bytes, or 1000 gigabytes

TPU (tensor processing unit): An application-specific integrated circuit developed by Google for machine learning

Training: See *model training*

Training data: The data used to fit the parameters of an analytic model

Unstructured data: Data such as free text or video that is not divided into predefined data fields

Version control system (VCS): A type of software tool that controls and archives changes to code, as well as other documents

XML (eXtensible Markup Language): A format for encoding data in a document that is both machine and human readable, as defined by certain standard specifications

Yottabyte: 10^{24} bytes, or 1000 zettabytes

Zettabyte: 10^{21} bytes, or 1000 exabytes

Index